Willi

By Michael W. Simmons

Copyright 2016 by Michael W. Simmons

Published by Make Profits Easy LLC

Profitsdaily123@aol.com

facebook.com/MakeProfitsEasy

Table of Contents

Introduction: Part One 4

Chapter One: An Obscure Birth 53

Chapter Two: The Lost Years: 1578-1582 71

Chapter Three: From Stratford to London 91

Chapter Four: Shakespeare's People 131

Chapter Five: Shakespeare at Home 161

Further Reading 174

Introduction: Part One

Why Shakespeare?

"It is sometimes suspected that the enthusiasm for Shakespeare's works shown by some students is a fiction or a fashion. It is not so. The justification of that enthusiastic admiration is in the fact that every increase of knowledge and deepening of wisdom in the critic or the student do but show still greater knowledge and deeper wisdom in the great poet. When, too, it is found that his judgment is equal to his genius, and that his industry is on a par with his inspiration, it becomes impossible to wonder or to admire too much."

George Dawson

Why do we still read Shakespeare today? In high school, you were probably forced to read, at minimum, one Shakespeare play, probably *Romeo and Juliet*, a story whose ending you already knew (and had seemingly always known). You may have gone on to read *Macbeth* or *King Lear* or *Hamlet* in the upper grades as well. What is it about these plays, written four centuries ago, that is so important that students are still forced to grapple with them in school?

Unfortunately, most people leave school without ever receiving a satisfactory answer to this question. The necessity of reading Shakespeare is taken for granted, by teachers as well as students. It isn't really good enough to say that the study of literature has always been considered a vital component of a well-rounded education; Shakespeare stands apart from most of the literature in the average high school literary curriculum. Apart from Chaucer, students are rarely required to read the work of any other writer whose time is so distant from our own, whose language is so unfamiliar as to scarcely seem like the English we grew up with. There is something about Shakespeare that has prevented him from sliding into the same obscurity as virtually every other writer of dramatic fiction prior to the invention of the novel. Even people who read for enjoyment rarely read plays. Apart from Shakespeare, no other playwright has enjoyed comparable levels of popularity in a printed format.

It may come as a gratifying surprise to some readers that even those people who go on to study literature in college, or otherwise pursue literature beyond the requirements of high school, are not always Shakespeare's biggest fans. What is special about Shakespeare is not always apparent, even to people who love books and reading. Early Modern English—the English of Shakespeare's time—poses a formidable obstacle to many readers, and with so many other more accessible writers to choose from, the fact that Shakespeare is considered as standing head and shoulders above the competition can seem curious. Is Shakespeare's reputation for genius merited, or is it simply a tradition—a meme repeated over generations, enduring only because to question it would be to question the authority of received wisdom?

In this book, you will be reading about the life of William Shakespeare, but first we should address the question of why Shakespeare is worth reading, and reading about. The premise of this text is that the body of work we consider to be the writing of William Shakespeare was indeed written by the actor from Stratford, and not by anyone else. We will address what is known as "the authorship question"—the belief, held by some people, that the true author of Hamlet, etc., was some other writer of the period, such as Christopher Marlowe or Edward de Vere or Francis Bacon—but the consensus here, as in the academic community at large, is that Shakespeare was Shakespeare, if for no other reason than because it makes for a more interesting story. There are many reasons to read about the life of Francis Bacon or the Earl of Oxford even if you don't think those men played any role in the authorship of Shakespeare's plays. There is no reason to read about William Shakespeare of Stratford, unless you understand him to be the author of the most extraordinary literature in the English language.

But why are Shakespeare's plays so extraordinary? Believe it or not, it's actually a brave question to ask. Shakespeare's genius is so taken for granted that it requires some nerve to admit that you don't actually understand what makes him such a big deal. This introductory essay is aimed at those readers who are curious about the answer to this question—that is, at casual readers of literature who feel at a loss to account for the enthusiasm that some of Shakespeare's most ardent admirers display at the most passing mention of his name. We will cover some context from the history of literature that will help you understand why Shakespeare was so different from the writers who came before him, and how literature ever since Shakespeare has been changed by his influence and example. First, however, we will begin where every reader begins: by opening the text of a play and grappling with the words on the page, exactly as they appear, without footnotes or historical references.

The language barrier

One secret that will help you understand what makes Shakespeare *Shakespeare* is time. Not the centuries of time that have passed since William Shakespeare trod the boards as a player at the Globe theater, but the time that the modern reader is willing to spend with his words.

It is, simply put, almost impossible for a 21st century reader who has never grappled with a version of English that is full of thee and thou to pick up a copy of, say, *Hamlet* and grasp all the nuance during their first reading. They will be lucky if they can keep the characters straight and remember the plot. Shakespeare's own contemporaries could and did manage it, but they had the advantage over us—Shakespeare was speaking in their vernacular.

The language barrier is the most forbidding obstacle that the average reader today has to contend with in appreciating what Shakespeare has to offer, and while there is no fast way to get around it, there is a simple way: read more slowly. Be prepared to be patient and take your time. It helps to read the dialogue out loud.

Shakespeare was writing, not for the solitary reader poring over a heavy book, but for the theater-goer, the audience member sitting (or, more likely, standing) below the stage, listening to the emphasis and inflection the actors bestowed on his lines. By reading the lines aloud, slowly, to yourself, you will find that you understand a great deal more Elizabethan English than you think you do. It isn't so different from ours, really. If you have ever had to read the King James Bible in church, for instance, you already have some practice grappling with the version of English that Shakespeare wrote in.

It is also strongly recommended that you watch a performance of the play you are reading, if at all possible, either live or on film. The dialogue of the play, the jokes and the insults especially, become immensely easier to understand once you have heard them spoken by a competent actor who knows where to place the proper emphasis and inflection. A good edition of Shakespeare will have footnotes that explain outdated references. For example: in Macbeth, there is a reference to "the poor cat i' the adage." The "adage" (saying) that Shakespeare is referring to is no longer a common saying amongst people today, so it's hardly the modern reader's fault if we don't understand the complexity of Lady Macbeth's insult. But if you watch this scene in the 1978 film of the playing starring Ian McKellen, and listen to Judi Dench deliver this line, it becomes no longer necessary to know the complete historical context of the proverb about the cat who wants to eat a fish but isn't willing to get her paws wet by snatching it out of the pond. The vitriol and contempt that is evident in the actress's tone of voice tells you everything you need to understand about the dynamic between the two characters in that scene.

The dramatic format

Another obstacle to the modern reader, besides the language barrier, is the fact that we simply aren't used to reading plays. We're accustomed to novels and short stories; hardly anyone reads poetry anymore, but there are still more people reading poetry than reading plays. When you are writing a story that will be told by actors on a stage, you make different choices than if you were writing a novel, or a movie script. Some of those choices will seem, frankly, weird to a reader who doesn't understand where they come from.

Most movies that you will have seen aspire to tell a story in a very natural style. The dialogue is supposed to sound as much like real conversation as possible; the actors' actions and movements bear a close resemblance to the way people act and move in real life. In movies, a lack of realism can be frustrating for the audience, and we tend to bring that same expectation to plays. Shakespeare, however, is in a strange in-between place, as far as realism in drama is concerned. He was much more like our modern movie-makers than anyone before him, but he was still telling stories through the conventions of the theater. This is why his characters sometimes do things that make very little sense to us, such as when Hamlet walks around on an otherwise empty stage and delivers a monologue. In real life, of course, no one does this; people do talk to themselves, but not in long, complex sentences with beautiful language that expresses fully-formed ideas. But consider this in the context of a theatrical performance. The actors performing these monologues were standing a long way off from most of the audience. Their faces and body language couldn't be seen clearly. An actor couldn't depend on the audience noticing the small nuances of their facial expressions, like an arched eyebrow or a wry smile. In movies, we rely on the fact that the camera is usually never very far away from the actors, especially during important emotional scenes. Characters don't have to tell us what they're thinking—we can intuit their thoughts and emotions for ourselves based on the way a muscle twitches in their jaw, or the way their hands clench into fists suddenly.

Shakespeare's characters were written with the understanding that, no matter how talented the actor portraying them might be, the text of the play itself would have to bear most of the responsibility for conveying to the audience the inner workings of the characters' minds. It feels unnatural to us, and in a way, it is. But when we accept the idea that we are being given privileged access to a character's inner life via the magic of theatrical conventions, we can devote our energy to task of getting to know that character intimately. And that is when we begin to experience Shakespeare in a way that makes it possible to understand why he is considered to be one of the most brilliant writers who ever lived, because the inner lives of his characters are complex, nuanced, and surprising.

Another theatrical convention that was common in Shakespeare's day can help us understand the plays even better, and that convention is audience participation. This may be the most striking difference between a live performance in

Shakespeare's time and live performances in our own time. These days, attending the theater is considered an eccentric hobby, a rare excursion for people with "refined" tastes, like going to the ballet, or the symphony. But in the Elizabethan era, a period during which theaters flourished, going to see a play was much more like going to see a movie is for us. Shakespeare and the other members of his theatrical company made most of their money through the sale of fairly cheap tickets, which were purchased by ordinary, common, "vulgar" people—the sort of people who expected risqué scenes and dirty jokes to play a significant role in their entertainment.

Theater audiences these days tend to sit quietly and sedately in their seats, passively watching the spectacle unfold before them. Elizabethan theater audiences were different. If a play was boring, they might very well throw things at the actors. More importantly, if an actor, alone on the stage, asked a question, the audience might very well answer them.

For example: in Act 2, Scene IV of *Measure for Measure*, the Duke's deputy, Angelo, has a conversation with Isabella, whose brother, Claudio, he has condemned to be executed. Angelo tells Isabella that he will spare Claudio's life—but only if she will have sex with him. Isabella is shocked and horrified; she's supposed to enter a convent and become a nun the very next day, and Angelo knows this. Furthermore, Angelo has a reputation for being the most pious, severely moral man in all of Vienna—that's why the Duke put him in charge. Not only is Angelo trying to coerce Isabella into committing fornication with him, but fornication is precisely the crime for which he's planning to have Claudio executed.

Outraged, Isabella declares to Angelo that, unless he signs a pardon for Claudio immediately, she will tell everyone in Vienna that he's a hypocrite, a sinner, and a breaker of the same laws he's enforcing on everyone else. But Angelo tells her that no one will believe her—and as soon as Isabella is alone again, she realizes that he's right. Alone on the stage, Isabella turns to the audience, and delivers the following monologue:

To whom should I complain? Did I tell this,
Who would believe me? O perilous mouths,
That bear in them one and the self-same tongue,
Either of condemnation or approof;
Bidding the law make court'sy to their will:
Hooking both right and wrong to the appetite,
To follow as it draws! I'll to my brother:

Though he hath fallen by prompture of the blood,
Yet hath he in him such a mind of honour.
That, had he twenty heads to tender down
On twenty bloody blocks, he'ld yield them up,
Before his sister should her body stoop
To such abhorr'd pollution.
Then, Isabel, live chaste, and, brother, die:
More than our brother is our chastity.
I'll tell him yet of Angelo's request,
And fit his mind to death, for his soul's rest.

In the first lines, Isabella echoes the horrible question Angelo first put to her: who will believe her? An Elizabethan audience would mostly have responded to this question, shouting back at the stage: "No one will believe you," they might have said, or "Tell the Duke!" By opening her inner thoughts to the audience, Isabella is asking a question of you, the reader: do you see what a predicament Isabella is in? Can you see why she feels so trapped, why she believes that she has no choice except to go to the prison and say goodbye to her brother? Shakespeare's characters were written for the purpose of drawing you into their story in this way.

Audience interaction wasn't limited solely to the monologues, either. Modern readers sometimes have difficulty appreciating the comic behavior of Shakespeare's clowns: characters like Feste, in

Twelfth Night, or Gobbo in *Merchant of Venice,* often don't seem especially funny to us. Humor is strongly dependent on social context, so it makes sense that we don't always get the punchlines of Elizabethan jokes. But Shakespeare's audience would have understood that the "fool" was more than just a comedian. The kings and queens of Europe, including Elizabeth I, still employed court jesters, and other wealthy people had fools in their own households. The job of the fool wasn't necessarily to perform acrobatic feats or wear ridiculous, brightly colored costumes, but to entertain his audience by any means necessary—sometimes by saying things that no one else dared to say. The fool was a stock character in the theater going back to Roman times, and while they provided comic relief, their role was also to nettle the audience into paying attention. Often they did this by engaging with the audience directly. Like a good modern stand-up comedian, they could take heckling from the audience and give as good as they got, to the point of jumping off stage and distracting theater-goers from a heavy emotional scene that had just taken place. A recent touring production of *Merchant of Venice* played along these lines—the actor playing Gobbo made a point of looking for the audience member in the first two rows who was laughing the loudest and drawing them into the scene, improvising and going off-script to keep the jokes going. If

Shakespeare's clowns don't seem especially clown-y to you, keep in mind that you may not be getting the full experience that Shakespeare's audiences would have been part of.

How Shakespeare changed literature

Another reason for Shakespeare's status in the world of literature is less easy to grasp, because Shakespeare, quite by accident, made it difficult to grasp. It is difficult for us to completely appreciate how original Shakespeare's works are because we live in the post-Shakespeare world. We are used to fictional characters whose motives are slippery, whose internal thoughts are chaotic, profound, funny, and tortured by turns. We're used to psychologically complex characters whose emotions and ideas influence their actions and drive the plot. What we don't realize—and how could we?—is that, when Shakespeare was writing, there was no precedent for this kind of characterization in dramatic fiction. The European novel had not yet been invented; writing, as we think of it today, did not exist as a profession. Shakespeare enjoyed great financial success from his writing, but he didn't make any money off of the sales of the printed volumes of his plays. In Shakespeare's time, no one really read Shakespeare. All his money came from ticket sales; if a play was not performed by actors in a theater, it made no money.

In other words, in the Elizabethan era, if you wanted to make your reputation as a writer, you didn't write dramatic fiction. You might write poetry, or what we now think of as creative nonfiction—essays, pamphlets, and books about history, religion, or philosophy. But a writer such as Shakespeare, who wrote for the enjoyment, principally, of common people, was not really regarded as a writer in the same way as the author of a learned tome on the Greek philosophers would have been. He was an entertainer. And yet, he essentially reinvented the writing of fictional characters. In fact, one of the most famous Shakespeare critics writing today asserts that Shakespeare was the inventor of what we now conceive of as the concept of "personality"—that all people have complex inner lives with an array of traits that are as unique to them as a fingerprint. It can be difficult for us to grasp what the world must have been like before it was so densely populated with fictional personalities that are sometimes as real to us as living people. But if you can grasp that it is Shakespeare we have to thank for virtually every memorable fictional character we've ever admired, you can begin to grasp why people still get terribly excited about him four hundred years after his death.

Before Shakespeare, the characters in a typical play were more like ciphers than human beings. They were defined by their rank and their role—they were a king, or a peasant, a witch or a mother, and little else. If you have ever seen a children's Christmas pageant, you have seen a somewhat watered-down example of what theater was like before Shakespeare. The children, dressed up as Mary, Joseph, angels, wise men, even donkeys and sheep, recite traditional dialogue that isn't meant to showcase the writer's talent or hint at psychological complexities within the characters or even be especially entertaining for the audience. The role of the dialogue is simply to tell the Christmas story. Plays were populated by stock characters: kings, queens, fools, peasants, virtuous maids and fallen women, noble youths and cowardly rogues. The dramatic emphasis of the story lay in the events that befell them, not the development of their feelings. A king might sit securely on his throne at the beginning of a play, only to be deposed and die at the end. The audience was entertained, because anything that happened to a king was interesting to everyone, but no one expected the king to undergo inner emotional changes, or for his emotional drama to fuel the plot.

Take *Antigone,* for instance, another play which you might have read in high school. In Sophocles' play, the king, Creon, forbids his niece, Antigone, from giving a proper burial to her brother, because he was a traitor to the throne. Antigone declares that she will perform the burial rites anyway, and at her first opportunity she does just that. Creon despoils her brother's grave again, and warns Antigone that if she disobeys his orders one more time, he will have her executed. She does it anyway. Creon walls her up alive in a cave; Antigone commits suicide, and so does her fiancé, Creon's son. Creon himself is left in ruins because of the consequences of his own actions. Sophocles' characters capture our sympathies because we can relate to their motivations, but they aren't especially complex, and we don't get to examine their decision-making processes. The dramatic tension of *Antigone* is created in part by the audience's awareness that Creon is setting himself up to suffer dreadful consequences by refusing to allow Antigone to honor the gods by performing the necessary funeral rites. Creon has ample opportunity to avoid those consequences, but he can't, for the simple reason that it isn't in the nature of characters in Greek plays to change their minds. Their fates are invariably determined by the unfortunate collision between their goals and the obstacles placed in their path. If you know the rules of pre-Shakespearean drama, you can make a pretty accurate guess as to what the fate of the characters will be as soon as the initial conflict is introduced. Creon warns Antigone that she will die if she buries her brother; Antigone buries her brother and dies. There isn't really a twist, so much as there is a building tension that only breaks when the worst comes to pass. People rarely get bored watching Sophocles' plays, but they're rarely surprised by the endings either.

Shakespeare made use of stock characters, but they were never merely stock characters. They were always individuals. The Greek dramatists, by contrast, were not especially interested in the individual. Antigone is an extraordinarily compelling character, but she is defined almost exclusively by what she is—that is, the daughter of a king. Her strength of will, her commitment to fulfill the demands of familial piety even at risk to her own life, are inherently royal virtues, and her function in the play is to act as the embodiment of those virtues. We don't really know how Antigone felt about her brothers. Did she love them both equally? One brother supported their uncle Creon's claim to the throne; the other attempted to take the throne for himself. Did Antigone support her rebellious brother's cause? We don't know, and as far as the play is concerned, the question is irrelevant. Individuals have favorites among their family members. Their love for one another is based on a variety of factors. But a king's daughter upholds duty to family over her private feelings.

If Shakespeare had written his own version of *Antigone*, it would have been a very different play. We would, at the very least, know more about Antigone's inner conflicts. Likewise, a Greek dramatist wouldn't have the first idea what to make of Hamlet. If Sophocles had written *Hamlet,* the play would have been much shorter. Hamlet probably would have spent half the play raising an army to take the throne of Denmark back from his uncle, and he would have killed Claudius at the end of the third act. The famous scene in which Hamlet hesitates to kill Claudius because he is praying would never have taken place. Hamlet would have been filled with a sense of the righteousness of his purpose; he wouldn't have hesitated to end the life of the man who killed his father, even if it did mean sending him to Heaven. But because Shakespeare wrote *Hamlet*, we have, not a play about a virtuous young man upholding his family's honor, but a play about a deeply troubled young man lost in his own mind, susceptible to fanciful fears, unable to reconcile his intense feelings about his father's death with his view of the world he inhabits. *Antigone and Hamlet* are both tragedies, but the tragedy stems from different sources in each. Sophocles drew his material from the conflict between opposing, immoveable forces: Antigone's piety and Creon's royal authority. Shakespeare drew from the nightmarish inner world of a fantastically flawed and imaginative person whose royal birth constitutes only one small portion of the forces that shape his actions. The leap from the impersonal to the personal is what sets Shakespeare apart.

This is why, when we are looking for an answer to the question, *Why do we read Shakespeare?* The best answer we can come up with is the simple fact that Shakespeare changed the world. It is thanks to Shakespeare that we can look to theater, movies, novels, and stories for insight into all that is changeable, mysterious, and elusive about human nature. And once we have recognized the enormity of his impact on our lives, we are inevitably moved to ask another question: what sort of person was Shakespeare? What was it that enabled him to make that revolutionary leap, to create characters that reflected aspects of the human experience never before seen onstage?

The problem of biography

The English, in Elizabethan times, were far more conscientious about record keeping than they had been in the medieval era, but not nearly to the degree that modern students of Shakespeare would wish. Most of the verifiable biographical details about Shakespeare that we possess today came to us only by dint of the dedicated historical detective work of Shakespeare scholars over the last four centuries. Although Shakespeare, almost uniquely for 16th century playwrights, was famous in his own lifetime, being a celebrity was a different sort of business back then. The man on the street, though he might know Shakespeare by name and be familiar enough with his work to quote entire speeches from *Henry IV* for the entertainment of his friends at the pub, would probably not have cared to know where Shakespeare was from, or how he'd got his start in the world of the London theater, or who his friends were, how he spent his leisure time, etc. Even though Shakespeare was regarded highly enough by his contemporaries that they collected his plays for publication after his death (which is the reason they survive to the present day), no one thought to write a "life" of the playwright. The fine details of his biography were not preserved for the edification of future generations.

For this reason, a large part of biographical scholarship pertaining to Shakespeare is inevitably based on conjecture. There are few facts to guide us; social and historical context supplies the rest. This would be frustrating in the case of any historical figure who continues to compel our interest today, but it is doubly so in Shakespeare's case, because we want to know one thing above all else: how did he do it? How did a man with a solid but limited grammar school education, a glover's son who probably never left England, whose entire world must have been limited to the haunts of his childhood in Stratford and the theatrical world of London, write so convincingly about kings and queens and battles and politics and history and all the rest of it?

There are two distinct periods of Shakespeare's life—the four years between the end of his formal education and his marriage to Anne Hathaway, and then the seven years between the birth of his twin children and the first mention of him in London's theatrical circles—about which we know nothing at all. Shakespeare scholars have attempted to trace his movements during these years, mostly by looking to his plays for clues. One theory supposes that he might have gone to Europe, where he visited Italy and learned the layout of the city of Venice, which would explain why Gobbo the clown is able to give such specific directions to Shylock's house in *The Merchant of Venice*. But there is no way to be certain that he ever did make such a journey, and more importantly, there is no single satisfactory theory about his activities during these years that would fully account for all the specific references and insights that appear in his plays.

The mystery of how Shakespeare was able to write what he wrote has tantalized scholars and amateurs alike for hundreds of years. Some people have gone so far as to conclude that there is no way that a man possessing the background and education of William Shakespeare of Stratford could have written all the plays attributed to him; in other words, that it is impossible for Shakespeare to actually be Shakespeare.

Part Two:

The Authorship Question

The debate surrounding the identity of the author of *Hamlet* and all the other plays credited to William Shakespeare is known as "the authorship question". Doubt was first cast on Shakespeare's authorship by a book which was published in 1848 by Joseph C. Hart, entitled *The Romance of Yachting,* in which Hart, whilst traveling in a part of the world that Shakespeare describes in *The Winter's Tale,* imagines how the construction of a fake Shakespearean identity might have come about:

"How prone the English people are to kill off their great men! They first raise them up to the loftiest pinnacle of fame, and then, like the eagle with the tortoise, or the monkey which mounts the highest tree with his cocoa-nut, they dash their victims 'all to pieces' upon the rocks below. Thus, also, they play the game of nine-pins with all their great statesmen. They set them up, ay, 'set them up, my boy!' for the pleasure of knocking them down. And then, again, they drink to the full, at the Castalian fount, and the inclination is irresistible to demolish the vessel that has served them:

'Sweet the pleasure

After drinking — to break glasses!'

"It is thus they have raised up Shakespeare; and now they are demolishing him, without remorse.

"After 'the bard' had been dead for one hundred years and utterly forgotten, a player and a writer of the succeeding century, turning over the old lumber of a theatrical "property-room," find bushels of neglected plays, and the idea of a "speculation" occurs to them. They dig at hazard and promiscuously, and disentomb the literary remains of many a "Wit" of a former century, educated men, men of mind, graduates of universities, yet starving at the door of some theatre, while their plays are in the hands of an ignorant and scurvy manager, awaiting his awful fiat. They die in poverty, and some of absolute starvation. Still their plays, to the amount of hundreds, remain in the hands of the manager, and become in some way or other his "property."

A 'factotum' is kept to revise, to strike out, to refit, revamp, interpolate, disfigure, to do any thing to please the vulgar and vicious taste of the multitude. No play will succeed, without it is well peppered with vulgarity and obscenity. The 'property-room' becomes lumbered to repletion with the efforts of genius.

"It was the fashion of the day for all literary men to write for the theatre. There was no other way to get their productions before the world. In the process of time, the brains of the "factotum," teeming with smut and overflowing all the while with prurient obscenity, the theatre becomes indicted for a nuisance, or it is sought to be "avoided" by the magistrates for its evil and immoral tendency. The managers are forced to retire; and one, who "owns all the properties," leaves the hundreds of original or interpolated plays to the usual fate of garret lumber, some with the supposed mark of his 'genius' upon them. They are useless to him, for he is a player and a manager no longer.

"A hundred years pass, and they and their reputed 'owner' are forgotten, and so are the poets who wrote and starved upon them. Then comes the resurrection — "on speculation." Betterton the player, and Rowe the writer, make a selection from a promiscuous heap of plays found in a garret, nameless as to authorship. 'I want a hero!' said Byron, when he commenced a certain poem. 'I want an author for this selection of plays!' said Rowe. 'I have it!' said Betterton; 'call them Shakespeare's!' And Rowe, the 'commentator' commenced to puff them as 'the bard's', and to 'write a history of his hero in which there was scarcely a word that had the foundation of truth to rest upon.'

"This is about the sum and substance of the manner of setting up Shakespeare: and the manner of pulling him down, may be gathered from the succeeding commentators — not one of whom, perhaps, dreamed of such a possibility while he was trying to immortalize his idol. But each one, as they succeeded one another, thought it necessary to outdo his predecessor in learning and research, and developed some startling antiquarian fact, which, by accumulation, worked the light of truth out of darkness, until, one after the other, the leaves of the chaplet, woven for Shakespeare "the immortal", fall, withered, to the ground; his monument, high as huge Olympus, crumbles into dust; and his apotheosis vanishes into thin air.

"Alas, Shakespeare! Lethe is upon thee! But if it drown thee it will give up and work the resurrection of better men and more worthy. Thou hast had thy century; they are about having theirs."

The above excerpt is a neat summary of many of the arguments made against William Shakespeare's authorship of the Shakespeare plays: the fact that Shakespeare was a relatively unknown name until the early eighteenth century, the fact that some of the plays seem to show evidence of having more than one contributor, and the difficulty writers had in being recognized or successful in the Elizabethan theatrical world. All of these factors seem, in Hart's eyes, to point to a kind of secret plot to pass the actor from Stratford off as the singular personality who miraculously produced a body of work that, realistically, must have been the work of many men.

The matter of Shakespeare's upbringing and education is a particular sticking-point for many anti-Stratfordians. In a later chapter of this book, we will examine in detail what sort of education Shakespeare probably received as a boy, but at this juncture, it is enough to say that some people believe it impossible for a person of Shakespeare's class and education to know all the things he would have needed to know to write the plays. Hart goes on to say,

"A writer in Lardner's Cabinet Cyclopoedia undertakes to give us the history of his family; from which I gather that John Shakespeare, the father of William, was very poor and very illiterate, notwithstanding what the ambitious commentators may say to the contrary. So says Lardner, and he proves it beyond dispute. The coat of arms and the heraldry obtained for the family, afterwards, was procured by fraud: and the proceeding is pronounced discreditable to 'the bard' who had a hand in it. But the poverty of the family is nothing in this case, except to show that William Shakespeare must necessarily have been an uneducated boy. He grew up in ignorance and viciousness, and became a common poacher — and the latter title, in literary matters, he carried to his grave. He was not the mate of the literary characters of the day, and no one knew it better than himself. It is a fraud upon the world to thrust his surreptitious fame upon it. He had none that was worthy of being transmitted. The enquiry will be, who were the able literary men who wrote the dramas imputed to him? The plays themselves, or rather a small portion of them, will live as long as

English literature is regarded worth pursuit. The authorship of the plays is no otherwise material to us, than as a matter of curiosity and to enable us to render exact justice; but they should not be assigned to Shakespeare alone, if at all."

Hart's assertion that Shakespeare was a "common poacher" in literary matters is fair, if somewhat prejudicial. Shakespeare made no bones about the fact that little of the material from which he drew the subjects of his plays was strictly original. He revised the plots of plays by other authors, such as *The Spanish Tragedy* by Thomas Kyd, which furnished some of the plot of *Hamlet*. Shakespeare borrowed deeply from a book published under the name of Raphael Holinshed, and entitled *The Chronicles of England, Scotland, and Ireland,* which was the most popular piece of historical scholarship written in the Tudor era. This supremely ambitious account of the history of the British Isles going back to the time of Noah's flood was actually the work of several men, organized by a publisher who hoped to write a similarly sweeping history of the whole world. Holinshed's *Chronicles* are divided into several volumes, and the average Englishman of the period probably drew whatever knowledge they possessed about the kings of England, Scotland, and Ireland from Holinshed's accounts.

Shakespeare's history plays, including *Henry VI*, parts 1-3, *Henry IV*, parts 1 and 2, *Richard II*, *Richard III*, *King John*, and *Henry VIII*, were all based on Holinshed's histories of the kings and historical events in question. (Plays such as *Antony and Cleopatra* and *Titus Andronicus*, though drawing from historical references, are considered tragedies rather than histories in Shakespearean terms; Shakespeare's history plays might more accurately be called British history plays.) Other works, such as *Macbeth and Cymbeline*, also build on information found in Holinshed.

The fact that Shakespeare drew so extensively from Holinshed and other sources, such as John Foxe's *Book of Martyrs*, is no argument against his originality, however, nor does it prove that he did not possess sufficient knowledge to write the plays attributed to him. For one thing, Shakespeare is very far from being the only writer who based their creative efforts on non-dramatic historical sources. Edmund Spenser, for instance, author of *The Faerie Queene*, a long dramatic poem written in part to flatter Elizabeth I, also drew from Holinshed.

But this idea, that Shakespeare was too common and too poorly educated to have possessed the mind that produced plays like *King Lear and Othello,* is the most common refrain to be found in the arguments of "anti-Stratfordians"—which is the name given to those who reject the authorship of William Shakespeare of Stratford. Though as many as eighty different candidates have been proposed as sole or partial authors of Shakespeare's work, almost all of the most popular candidates have in common a university education and aristocratic birth. At present, the favorite contenders for Shakespeare's title are Edward de Vere, Earl of Oxford, Francis Bacon, and Christopher Marlowe, with a small but vocal minority advocating for Elizabeth I. The reasoning for the secrecy surrounding their authorship of the plays resembles a conspiracy theory. Because de Vere and Bacon both occupied delicate positions in the court of Elizabeth I, it is thought that they used playwriting as a means of criticizing the queen and her royal ancestors, but dared not risk letting her find out that such criticism came from their pens. Elizabeth herself, supposedly, feared that the writing of plays would be considered unbecoming of her sex. The playwright Christopher Marlowe, somewhat more excitingly, is thought to have been a spy who faked his death in a tavern brawl. Supposedly, he borrowed the name of his friend and fellow actor, William Shakespeare, in order to continue writing without arousing suspicion that he was still alive.

Edward de Vere, the Earl of Oxford, is currently the most popular of all the "alternative Shakespeare" candidates. A courtier and sometime favorite of Elizabeth I, his advocates claim that there are a number of biographical allusions in the Shakespeare plays that correspond to events in his own life. There are a few problems that have to be reckoned with in the Oxfordian version of events, however; for instance, several of Shakespeare's best plays, including *Macbeth*, were written after de Vere died. Furthermore, de Vere wasn't at all shy about criticizing the queen. In fact, he spent more time away from her court than he did in dancing attendance upon her, because he felt that she did not grant him favors in accordance with his merits. Performances of *Richard II* were banned by Elizabeth I because of the scene in which the king abdicates his throne. As a courtier, de Vere would have been well aware that Elizabeth feared that Parliament might call for her abdication in favor of a female relative who was married and could produce male heirs. It is unlikely he would have made such a gaffe. William Shakespeare, on the other hand, had his understanding of royal personalities from history books, not from extended court sessions in the presence of the reigning queen; it would have been easy for him to make such a political misstep.

Sir Francis Bacon was the first person to be suggested as a plausible "true" author of Shakespeare's plays. Shortly after the publication of *The Romance of Yachting,* American writers and intellectuals, led by Delia Bacon, took up the Baconian cause, publishing a number of books and essays on the subject. Certain of Bacon's partisans even claim that the plays of Shakespeare contain a secret code which Bacon used to assert his identity as their author. A Bacon authorship presents some of the same problems as the de Vere authorship, however; Bacon occupied only a minor position at Elizabeth's court, and was often out of her favor. He was a conscientious opponent of Elizabeth's subsidies bill while he was serving as a member of Parliament for Middlesex; it seems likely that he had all the outlet he needed for voicing criticisms of her policies.

As to Elizabeth herself, it can at least be said that she was a talented poet in her own right. Her romantic poem, On *Monsieur's Departure,* is one of the finest of the era. But a cursory study of Elizabeth's life as queen will reveal that she simply had no time in which to produce a body of work like Shakespeare's. She was no figurehead queen; she was extremely dedicated to managing affairs of state, to the point of plaguing her advisors with demands that they return to court in the middle of the night to answer her questions. Furthermore, having been controlled by powerful men all her life, she chose not to marry, despite the fact that all of her advisors, and all of Parliament, were perpetually badgering her to do just that. While she outwardly extolled the virtues of wifely obedience to husbands, she made a point of avoiding marriage so that she might retain supreme authority as queen. It is extremely difficult to imagine such a person as the author of a play like *The Taming of the Shrew*.

Christopher Marlowe's case for the authorship of Shakespeare's plays is, perhaps, the strongest of the four leading contenders. De Vere's advocates do not properly account for the fact that he predeceased Shakespeare, and thus the writing of several of his plays, by a full decade. Marlowe's advocates at least attempt to explain the inconvenient matter of Marlowe's dying shortly before the first of Shakespeare's plays were introduced to the public; in fact, that is among their strongest arguments for Marlowe's authorship, since William Shakespeare of

Stratford's transformation from actor to playwright occurred at about the same time that Marlowe died—or rather, faked his death and found himself in need of a new identity, according to the theory. Furthermore, it is fairly incontrovertible that Shakespeare copied, or at least, intentionally emulated, Marlowe's verse style at various points throughout his plays. This can be seen in the opening lines of what was probably Shakespeare's first play, 1 Henry VI, as well as in the famous lines from *Romeo and Juliet,*

"But soft! What light through yonder window breaks?

It is the East, and Juliet is the sun!"

which bear an inarguable resemblance to Marlowe's lines from *The Jew of Malta,*

"But stay! What star shines yonder in the east?

The lodestar of my life, if Abigail!"

But as any writer who has worked in close concert with a fellow writer will assert, it is difficult, if not impossible, for such colleagues to avoid imitating one another. It is even possible that Shakespeare admired Marlowe and intentionally copied his style because he considered Marlowe the superior writer. Marlowe died in 1593, at the very beginning of Shakespeare's writing career. Marlow was already a successful, established, and widely admired writer of verse when Shakespeare was just starting out; in fact, some critics today consider it possible that, had Marlowe lived as long as Shakespeare, he might well have matured into a dramatist of equal or superior abilities. Nonetheless, it is difficult to imagine why Marlowe would have maintained the ruse of his death for over twenty years. A much simpler explanation of events is simply that he was dead in truth.

In the words of one anti-Stratfordian, to believe in the authorship of Edward de Vere or Francis Bacon or Christopher Marlowe, you must believe in a conspiracy of silence that spanned twenty years and reached as high as Queen Elizabeth herself; but to believe in the authorship of William Shakespeare, you must believe in miracles. The thing is, however, when genius like Shakespeare's appears in the world, it always strikes us as miraculous, and such a talent would not necessarily have been less of a miracle if it had presented itself in the form of a university educated gentleman of noble birth. There are any number of men and women who were contemporaries of Shakespeare who were more conveniently positioned to acquire intimate knowledge of life inside the royal court, but it does not follow that they would have known what to do with the insights they possessed, even if playwriting had been an interest of theirs. A talent like Shakespeare's, which was capable of bringing human beings to life on the stage in a way never seen before, was more than capable of intuiting those secret tics and doubts that people of royal and noble birth only entertained in private. There is, indeed, almost a kind of snobbishness at the back of anti-Stratfordian sentiments, as if the very idea of someone of common birth presuming to know the minds of his betters (and worse, presuming with an accuracy that looks like first-hand knowledge) was so offensive as to be ludicrous.

While the authorship question continues to titillate the imaginations of certain people, the consensus of the academic community is that there is no genuine evidence for and no validity to the authorship claims of any person other than William Shakespeare of Stratford. And yet, the anti-Stratfordian perspective has had some famous and highly respect adherents—including

Mark Twain, whose short book, *Is Shakespeare Dead?,* appeared some fifty years after *The Romance of Yachting* was published and the first questions about the authorship of the plays had been raised. The following long excerpt, taken from the third chapter of the book, is presented without commentary; it deserves to be the last word on the authorship question, at least for the purposes of this introduction, because it has the virtue of being both funny and accurate. All the charges which the author of *Tom Sawyer* lays to Shakespeare's account are true: very little is known about him, and what is known does not necessarily explain or support the idea that he was an artistic genius. Twain presents these charges to bolster his claim that Shakespeare's plays were not written by him; he claims of Shakespeare that, "He is a brontosaur: nine bones and six hundred barrels of plaster." But the paucity of verifiable biographical data about Shakespeare is a fact that must be contended with, whether one is pro- or anti-Stratfordian, and Twain sums them up as neatly as could be wished:

"How curious and interesting is the parallel — as far as poverty of biographical details is concerned — between Satan and Shakespeare. It is wonderful, it is unique, it stands quite alone, there is nothing resembling it in history, nothing resembling it in romance, nothing approaching it even in tradition.

How sublime is their position, and how over-topping, how sky-reaching, how supreme — the two Great Unknowns, the two Illustrious Conjecturabilities! They are the best-known unknown persons that have ever drawn breath upon the planet.

"For the instruction of the ignorant I will make a list, now, of those details of Shakespeare's history which are FACTS— verified facts, established facts, undisputed facts.

"Facts:

"He was born on the 23d of April, 1564.

"Of good farmer-class parents who could not read, could not write, could not sign their names.

"At Stratford, a small back settlement which in that day was shabby and unclean, and densely illiterate. Of the nineteen important men charged with the government of the town, thirteen had to "make their mark" in attesting important documents, because they could not write their names.

"Of the first eighteen years of his life NOTHING is known. They are a blank.
On the 27th of November (1582) William Shakespeare took out a license to marry Anne Whateley.

"Next day William Shakespeare took out a license to marry Anne Hathaway. She was eight years his senior.

"William Shakespeare married Anne Hathaway. In a hurry. By grace of a reluctantly granted dispensation there was but one publication of the banns.

Within six months the first child was born.

"About two (blank) years followed, during which period NOTHING AT ALL HAPPENED TO SHAKESPEARE, so far as anybody knows.

"Then came twins — 1585. February.

"Two blank years follow.

"Then — 1587 — he makes a ten-year visit to London, leaving the family behind.

Five blank years follow. During this period NOTHING HAPPENED TO HIM, as far as anybody actually knows.

"Then — 1592 — there is mention of him as an actor.

"Next year — 1593 — his name appears in the official list of players.

"Next year — 1594 — he played before the queen. A detail of no consequence: other obscurities did it every year of the forty-five of her reign. And remained obscure.

Three pretty full years follow. Full of play-acting. Then:

"In 1597 he bought New Place, Stratford.

"Thirteen or fourteen busy years follow; years in which he accumulated money, and also reputation as actor and manager.

"Meantime his name, liberally and variously spelt, had become associated with a number of great plays and poems, as (ostensibly) author of the same.

"Some of these, in these years and later, were pirated, but he made no protest.

"Then — 1610–11 — he returned to Stratford and settled down for good and all, and busied himself in lending money, trading in tithes, trading in land and houses; shirking a debt of forty-one shillings, borrowed by his wife during his long desertion of his family; suing debtors for shillings and coppers; being sued himself for shillings and coppers; and acting as confederate to a neighbor who tried to rob the town of its rights in a certain common, and did not succeed.

"He lived five or six years — till 1616 — in the joy of these elevated pursuits. Then he made a will, and signed each of its three pages with his name.

"A thoroughgoing business man's will. It named in minute detail every item of property he owned in the world — houses, lands, sword, silver-gilt bowl, and so on — all the way down to his "second-best bed" and its furniture.

"It carefully and calculatingly distributed his riches among the members of his family, overlooking no individual of it. Not even his wife: the wife he had been enabled to marry in a hurry by urgent grace of a special dispensation before he was nineteen; the wife whom he had left husbandless so many years; the wife who had had to borrow forty-one shillings in her need, and which the lender was never able to collect of the prosperous husband, but died at last with the money still lacking. No, even this wife was remembered in Shakespeare's will.

"He left her that 'second-best bed.'

"And NOT ANOTHER THING; not even a penny to bless her lucky widowhood with.

"It was eminently and conspicuously a business man's will, not a poet's.

"It mentioned NOT A SINGLE BOOK.

"Books were much more precious than swords and silver-gilt bowls and second-best beds in those days, and when a departing person owned one he gave it a high place in his will.

"The will mentioned NOT A PLAY, NOT A POEM, NOT AN UNFINISHED LITERARY WORK, NOT A SCRAP OF MANUSCRIPT OF ANY KIND.

"Many poets have died poor, but this is the only one in history that has died THIS poor; the others all left literary remains behind. Also a book. Maybe two.

"If Shakespeare had owned a dog — but we not go into that: we know he would have mentioned it in his will. If a good dog, Susanna would have got it; if an inferior one his wife would have got a downer interest in it. I wish he had had a dog, just so we could see how painstakingly he would have divided that dog among the family, in his careful business way.

"He signed the will in three places.

"In earlier years he signed two other official documents.

"These five signatures still exist.

"There are NO OTHER SPECIMENS OF HIS PENMANSHIP IN EXISTENCE. Not a line.

"Was he prejudiced against the art? His granddaughter, whom he loved, was eight years old when he died, yet she had had no teaching, he left no provision for her education, although he was rich, and in her mature womanhood she couldn't write and couldn't tell her husband's manuscript from anybody else's — she thought it was Shakespeare's.

"When Shakespeare died in Stratford, IT WAS NOT AN EVENT. It made no more stir in England than the death of any other forgotten theater-actor would have made. Nobody came down from London; there were no lamenting poems, no eulogies, no national tears — there was merely silence, and nothing more. A striking contrast with what happened when Ben Jonson, and Francis Bacon, and Spenser, and Raleigh, and the other distinguished literary folk of Shakespeare's time passed from life! No praiseful voice was lifted for the lost Bard of Avon; even Ben Jonson waited seven years before he lifted his.

"SO FAR AS ANYBODY ACTUALLY KNOWS AND CAN PROVE, Shakespeare of Stratford-on-Avon never wrote a play in his life.
SO FAR AS ANY ONE KNOWS, HE RECEIVED ONLY ONE LETTER DURING HIS LIFE.

"So far as any one KNOWS AND CAN PROVE, Shakespeare of Stratford wrote only one poem during his life. This one is authentic. He did write that one — a fact which stands undisputed; he wrote the whole of it; he wrote the whole of it out of his own head. He commanded that this work of art be engraved upon his tomb, and he was obeyed. There it abides to this day. This is it:

"'Good friend for Iesus sake forbeare To digg the dust encloased heare: Blest be ye man yt spares thes stones And curst be he yt moves my bones.'"

"In the list as above set down will be found EVERY POSITIVELY KNOWN fact of Shakespeare's life, lean and meager as the invoice is. Beyond these details we know NOT A THING about him. All the rest of his vast history, as furnished by the biographers, is built up, course upon course, of guesses, inferences, theories, conjectures — an Eiffel Tower of artificialities rising sky-high from a very flat and very thin foundation of inconsequential facts."

The facts cannot be argued with. It is as Twain says; Shakespeare disappears from view for much of his life, and those details that can be verified are related primarily to his financial transactions. These facts are scarcely definitive, however; there are many answers that could be made to Twain's assertions.

For instance, regarding the charge that Shakespeare made no effort to teach his granddaughter (or, in fact, his daughters) to read, it must be remembered that literacy was not considered a necessary skill for people in their station in life, particularly for women. In fact, it was not uncommon for women to be illiterate up until the beginning of the 20th century. And regarding the charge that Shakespeare made no provision for his plays, manuscripts, or poems in his will—Twain may not have been aware that intellectual property law was not the same in the early 17th century. The bulk of the profit for any publication returned to the man who undertook the trouble and expense of getting it printed; the author of the publication was lucky to see profits of any kind. Shakespeare made money from his plays by having them performed and selling tickets to the performances. The pages on which the play was written would have been almost as valueless to him and his family as they were to others. When Ben Jonson and others had Shakespeare's plays collected and printed in what is now known as the First Folio, a few years after his death, Shakespeare's family made no effort to collect any money from the sales; this must surely indicate to us that the Shakespeare family had no reason to believe they were entitled to any of those funds.

And as to Shakespeare's leaving the "second best bed" to his wife—in the Elizabethan era, the second best bed was generally the marriage bed, while the better bed was reserved for guests. So, as bequests go, it might not have been as unpoetic and unsentimental as Twain seems to have believed.

Speaking of Ben Jonson; he was contemporary with Shakespeare, and is considered to have been the best writer of his era apart from Shakespeare. It is interesting that Jonson remained a celebrated and widely-read author for the century following his death—a century in which Shakespeare's name became virtually unknown. Jonson himself would probably have been surprised by this disposition of their reputations. No one ever accused Jonson of being a beard for the "true author" of his own writing—and yet, it is from this superior literary talent that we receive history's first panegyric on Shakespeare and his memory. Jonson must certainly have been part of the conspiracy, if the anti-Stratfordians are right about there having been one. Jonson tells us plainly, in the poem he wrote for the publication of the First Folio, that he considered Shakespeare to be a writer without peer. Shakespeare's famous lack of education, such a sticking-point for anti-Stratfordians, Jonson acknowledged openly—yet Jonson also acknowledges that his "small Latin and less Greek" did not prevent him from becoming "the applause, delight, the wonder of our stage!"

Perhaps the last word of all on the authorship question should go to Jonson, since, unlike most people who have weighed in on the subject, Jonson knew Shakespeare personally, and was probably better equipped even than Mark Twain to judge whether the man from Stratford was capable of writing the plays that bear his name. The following is the complete text of Jonson's poem, "To the Memory of My Beloved, the Author, Mr. William Shakespeare and What He Hath Left Us", originally printed as a prefix to the First Folio:

To draw no envy, Shakespeare, on thy name,
Am I thus ample to thy book and fame;
While I confess thy writings to be such
As neither man nor muse can praise too much;
'Tis true, and all men's suffrage. But these ways
Were not the paths I meant unto thy praise;
For seeliest ignorance on these may light,
Which, when it sounds at best, but echoes right;
Or blind affection, which doth ne'er advance
The truth, but gropes, and urgeth all by chance;
Or crafty malice might pretend this praise,
And think to ruin, where it seem'd to raise.
These are, as some infamous bawd or whore

Should praise a matron; what could hurt her more?
But thou art proof against them, and indeed,
Above th' ill fortune of them, or the need.
I therefore will begin. Soul of the age!
The applause, delight, the wonder of our stage,
My Shakespeare, rise! I will not lodge thee by
Chaucer, or Spenser, or bid Beaumont lie
A little further, to make thee a room:
Thou art a monument without a tomb,
And art alive still, while thy book doth live,
And we have wits to read, and praise to give.
That I not mix thee so, my brain excuses;
I mean, with great but disproportion'd Muses.
For, if I thought my judgment were of years,
I should commit thee, surely, with thy peers.
And tell how far thou didst our Lyly outshine,
Or sporting Kyd, or Marlowe's mighty line.
And though thou hadst small Latin and less Greek,
From thence, to honour thee, I would not seek
For names; but call forth thund'ring Aeschylus,
Euripides, and Sophocles to us,
Paccuvius, Accius, him of Cordova dead
To life again, to hear thy buskin tread
And shake a stage; or when thy socks were on,
Leave thee alone, for the comparison
Of all that insolent Greece or haughty Rome
Sent forth; or since did from their ashes come.
Triumph, my Britain! Thou hast one to show
To whom all scenes of Europe homage owe.
He was not of an age, but for all time!
And all the Muses still were in their prime,
When, like Apollo, he came forth to warm

Our ears, or, like a Mercury, to charm.
Nature herself was proud of his designs,
And joy'd to wear the dressing of his lines,
Which were so richly spun, and woven so fit
As, since, she will vouchsafe no other wit.

Chapter One: An Obscure Birth

Born into troubled times

The precise date of William Shakespeare's birthday is unknown, nor can it be determined with certainty. His birth was recorded in the baptismal register of Holy Trinity Church in Stratford, England, on April 26, 1564, but the birth likely took place a few days before—two or three days' wait was customary.

In 1564, England was in the midst of serious religious upheaval. Elizabeth I had been crowned Queen only a few years before; she was preceded by her sister, Mary I, her brother, Edward VI, and her father, Henry VIII, all of whom had contributed to the turmoil of the Catholic-versus-Protestant wars of the late 16th century. In 1533, King Henry had overthrown the Catholic church in England in order to divorce his first wife, Katherine of Aragon, and marry Lady Anne Boleyn. Henry's son, Edward, educated in the fashion of the new Reformed religion, upheld Protestantism when he came to the throne in 1547. King Edward's religious reforms included continuing his father's Settlement Acts, which seized the funds and properties of Catholic monasteries and other institutions for the State. Some of these funds were channeled into King Edward VI Grammar Schools, free and independently endowed schools that offered good educations to poor boys who could keep up with the work. One such school was located in Stratford, and it is there that Shakespeare received his early education.

King Edward was succeeded by his Catholic sister Mary in 1553, who attempted to restore the old religion in England by persecuting Protestants as heretics. Her reign was short, however, and when Elizabeth I came to the throne in 1559, fortunes reversed for Catholics again. In Elizabeth's reign, Catholics were not prosecuted for heresy, but they were implicated in a number of plots to deprive the Protestant Elizabeth of her throne; rosaries, crucifixes, and icons would be made illegal, and attendance at Protestant services was made mandatory, with "recusants" penalized by a small fine.

The Book of Common Prayer, published during Edward's reign and established as the official order of services in English churches when Elizabeth's Act of Uniformity was passed in 1559, called for children to be baptized on the first Sunday or feast day after the child's birth. Today,

Shakespeare's birthday is celebrated on April 23rd, three days before his baptism. Shakespeare biographer Daniel Kay points out that "if Shakespeare was indeed born on Sunday, April 23, the next feast day would have been St. Mark's Day on Tuesday the twenty-fifth... St. Mark's Day was still held to be unlucky, as it had been before the Reformation, when altars and crucifixes used to be draped in black cloth, and when some claimed to see in the churchyard the spirits of those doomed to die in that year." This may explain why the christening was postponed until the 26th. In any event, April the 23rd is the most popular date assigned to Shakespeare's birth partly because it is also the day on which he is thought to have died in 1616.

The Shakespeare family

What we know of Shakespeare's family tree, we owe mostly to an application filed by his father when he was seeking a coat of arms. John Shakespeare was a glover and tanner, a craftsman who made leather goods, but he asserted that his grandfather had fought for the Tudors in the Battle of Bosworth Field, and that he had been awarded land by royal warrant for his bravery. Whether or not this is true, no one can say, but it is known that John's father,

Richard, was a tenant farmer who occasionally got into trouble with the law. Shakespeare's mother Mary, however, was descended from an aristocratic family by the name of Arden. Her grandfather was the owner of a large property, some of which was willed to Mary on her father's death, an estate called Asbies which John Shakespeare mortgaged in 1579.

John and Mary Shakespeare had a total of eight children during the course of their marriage: Joan, born in 1558, Margaret in 1562, William in 1564, Gilbert in 1566, a second daughter named Joan in 1569, Anne in 1571, Richard in 1574, and Edmund in 1580.

The elder Joan and Margaret both died before the age of one, and William was thus an only child for two years, until Gilbert was born. Gilbert lived to be forty-six, and had a successful career as a haberdasher in Stratford. Following him was Joan, the first surviving daughter and the longest-lived of all Shakespeare's family: she was seventy-seven when she died, and her son would become a well-known actor in the 17th century, specializing in performing roles written by his uncle, particularly Falstaff. The next child, Anne, died at the age of eight; the cause of death is not known, but plague, cholera, typhoid, sweating sickness, and other diseases routinely killed people in large numbers during the summers, and she might have died from any of these. Of Shakespeare's brother Richard, nothing is known, save that he died in 1613 at the age of thirty-nine.

Shakespeare's youngest sibling, Edmund, who was sixteen years his junior, followed his older brother to London to become an actor. He died there at the age of twenty-seven, probably of disease. According to Amanda Mabillard,

"He was buried in St. Saviour's Church, in Southwark, on December 31 of that year. His funeral was costly and magnificent, with tolling bells heard across the Thames. It is most likely that William planned the funeral for his younger brother because he would have been the only Shakespeare wealthy enough to afford such an expensive tribute to Edmund. In addition, records show that the funeral was held in the morning, and as Dennis Kay points out, funerals were usually held in the afternoon. It is probable that the morning funeral was arranged so that Shakespeare's fellow actors could attend the burial of Edmund."

Shakespeare would have three children of his own, two of whom survived to adulthood (an impressive percentage, considering that the infant mortality rate at the time was around 14% of all children under the age of one). Neither of Shakespeare's daughters would have children of their own, however. As a result, it is believed that Shakespeare's direct line died off in the early 17th century. However, it is rumored that Joan Shakespeare's son, William, had an illegitimate son by the name of Charles Hart, who was an especially famous actor during the reign of Charles II. William Hart was also a well known-actor, who specialized in performing roles which were written by his uncle.

Of the few facts which are known about Shakespeare's parents, one which stands out for its poignancy is that John Shakespeare applied for a coat of arms in the year 1570, when his son William was six years old. A successful application would have granted him the right to style himself a gentleman. However, John Shakespeare either failed in his petition or dropped it suddenly, without explanation.

Shakespeare's father was a fairly important man in Stratford, occupying a number of civic offices which would have distinguished him in a small independent town. When his son William was a young child, John Shakespeare was bailiff—a position roughly equivalent to that of mayor, but with far more extensive powers—and chief alderman, empowered to order arrests and otherwise manage the civil peace in Stratford. For him to seek the rank of gentleman was not an overreach of his dignity. There is some speculation that John Shakespeare might have been Catholic, which would explain a great deal about his sudden reversal of fortune in the late 1570's. Being Catholic, or having close Catholic family members, was politically ruinous at the time. Speculation about John Shakespeare's religion is based on the fact that he was fined, in 1592, for failure to attend church. There were a number of such "recusants" in England in the mid-to-late 16th century—Elizabeth I had made attendance at Protestant churches mandatory, and the modest fine for non-attendance (which was often not collected) was most often levied against conscientious Catholics who practiced their religion in private. While it was safer to be a Catholic in Elizabeth's reign than it had been to be a Protestant under Mary's, it still was not a predictor of civic prosperity.

But there is also evidence that the reason John Shakespeare had ceased attending church was because he feared he would be arrested for debt if he appeared in public. This was around the same time that his name was struck from the rolls of aldermen, after a long period of non-attendance at meetings. Considering how well John Shakespeare had married, and how prosperous he had once been, something serious seems to have happened to make him stop participating in his civic duties, and fall into debt. This may have been related to business setbacks, but the blow must have been profound, because he never recovered from them. It wasn't until William Shakespeare had begun to enjoy a degree of fame and success in London in the early 1590's that John Shakespeare's fortunes began to improve again, and by then he was very near the end of his life.

The education of William Shakespeare

If there was a defining moment in William Shakespeare's childhood which set him on the path to making a career as a writer, rather than a skilled craftsman of some sort like his father and brothers, it was probably when he became a student at the famous King Edward grammar school in Stratford at the age of six. There is no formal record of Shakespeare's time there, and not every boy in Stratford had access to the school, which had been in operation for over two hundred years already by the time Shakespeare would have been old enough to attend. (The King Edward grammar schools were established across England by Elizabeth I's younger brother, but in the case of the Stratford school, the royal warrant was simply extended to a school which had been founded by Stratford's famous guild in centuries past.) But John Shakespeare's position as an alderman would have made William eligible to attend, and it is difficult to imagine how Shakespeare could have attained the education that is evident from his writing unless he had taken advantage of this opportunity.

Shakespeare probably received his first lessons in reading from a "hornbook"—a sheet of paper, printed with the alphabet, basic lessons in phonics, and the Lord's Prayer, which was attached to a piece of wood and covered with a clear sheet of horn, to protect it so that it could be reused by younger students when pupils had finished memorizing it. The education of most literate children in the 16th and early 17th centuries began with hornbooks.

The primary purpose of the school was to instill the boys who studied there with a working knowledge of Latin. It is difficult to over-emphasize the importance of Latin in the

Elizabethan era. It was, in a sense, still a living language then; Latin was the language of state matters, and all official documents. It was the language which united Christendom, and until the Act of Uniformity was passed in England, it was the language of religion itself. Elizabeth I spoke Latin fluently, to the point that she could make casual conversation in that language with foreign ambassadors who did not speak English (or any of the other six or seven languages which Elizabeth spoke.) Gaining fluency in Latin was, in essence, the entire point of getting an education, especially for people of Shakespeare's class. A knowledge of Latin could be a ticket to upward social mobility, something which had only just become possibly in England, which was transitioning from a medieval, feudal society into a society with a merchant-driven middle class. It is, therefore, not especially strange that John Shakespeare, who might have been able to read a bit but probably could not write, would wish for William to attend school; he would have recognized that such an education might enable his oldest son to better his lot.

According to Shakespeare scholar Stephen Greenblatt,

"By statute, the Stratford schoolmaster was not allowed to take money for his instruction from any of the students. He was to teach any male child who qualified—that is, anyone who had learned the rudiments of reading and writing—'be their parents never so poor and the boys never so unapt'. For this he received free housing and an annual salary of twenty pounds, a substantial sum at the high end of what Elizabethan schoolmasters could hope to make. The town of Stratford was serious about the education of its children: after the free grammar school there were special scholarships to enable promising students of limited means to attend university. This was not, to be sure, universal free education... The sons of the very poor...did not go to school, for they were expected to begin work at a young age, and besides, though there was no fee, there were some expenses: students were expected to bring quills for pens, a knife for sharpening the quills, candles in winter, and—an expensive commodity—paper. But for the sons of families of some means, however modest, a rigorous education, centered on the classics, was accessible."

Shakespeare's earliest biographer—Nicholas Rowe, of whom Joseph C. Hart spoke so slightingly in *The Romance of Yachting*—claims that Shakespeare was forced to leave the grammar school through family necessity of some kind when he was thirteen, and in the absence of positive evidence to the contrary, scholars accept this theory. Considering that Ben Jonson made a point of informing his readers about Shakespeare's "small Latin", it does seem likely that either Shakespeare did not complete the full course of his education at the grammar school, or that he was a rather indifferent student.

Shakespeare's childhood—and indeed, the whole of his youth up to his marriage—is one of the "dark" periods of his life, concerning which there is virtually no verified information about his activities to be found. Based on the pedagogical theory prevalent at the time, however, it can be reasonably conjectured that Shakespeare took part in the staging of amateur theatricals while at school. Performing plays written in Latin by classical authors such as Plautus was considered one of the best means of instilling Latin in students. (The other chief method of insuring that lessons were retained was to beat the students with a rod when they made mistakes.) Latin plays were such a cornerstone of the average schoolboy's education that John Foxe, author of an epic work of Protestant propaganda known as Foxe's *Book of Martyrs,* wrote a number of original plays in Latin while he was in university. This training in dramatic fiction is evident in *Martyrs,* which had a profound influence on Shakespeare's early plays in the *Henry VI* cycle.

It is probably worth noting that, according to some of the same educational authorities who recommended amateur dramatics as a means of promoting Latin learning, there was a distinct danger in allowing the students to act out love scenes. Girls were not permitted to be students in school any more than women were permitted to be actresses in the theater, so even the most innocent theatrical love scenes were tainted by a hint of illicit homosexuality. These authorities warned earnestly against the danger of allowing schoolboys to kiss one another in the guise of dramatic characters—the danger, of course, being that some latent homosexual tendency would be awakened in the students as a result of the experience, which would inevitably lead to their ruin. This is intriguing to scholars who have long speculated about Shakespeare's sexuality. T*he Merchant of Venice* and *Troilus* and *Cressida* both have characters who are arguably gay; more importantly, several of Shakespeare's most famous sonnets are addressed to beloved objects who are unambiguously male, and his sonnets are dedicated to a "Mr. W.H.", who has traditionally been associated with the "fair youth" who appears in Sonnet 18, and others:

Shall I compare thee to a summer's day?
Thou art more lovely and more temperate:
Rough winds do shake the darling buds of May,
And summer's lease hath all too short a date:
Sometime too hot the eye of heaven shines,
And often is his gold complexion dimm'd;
And every fair from fair sometime declines,
By chance, or nature's changing course, untrimm'd;
But thy eternal summer shall not fade
Nor lose possession of that fair thou ow'st;
Nor shall Death brag thou wander'st in his shade,
When in eternal lines to time thou grow'st;
So long as men can breathe or eyes can see,
So long lives this, and this gives life to thee.

There is no way to be certain that Shakespeare felt sexual attraction towards men, of course, but in every area of historical scholarship, it pays to keep in mind that homosexuality has always been present, and has usually been erased. Certainly, the educational authorities of Shakespeare's day would not have felt so strongly that the awakening of homosexual impulses was something to be guarded against, if not for the fact that some people, inevitably, succumbed to them.

As for other theatrical experiences which Shakespeare may have had as a boy, it is also known that when Shakespeare was small, his father, as the bailiff of Stratford (an office equivalent to that of mayor), authorized payments to traveling theatrical troupes who made their way into town. For a child in a sleepy village in southern England, this would have been a momentous occasion, an unexpected source of entertainment unlike any he had witnessed before. The early and no doubt vivid impression that these players would likely have made upon the five or six year old William probably sparked his initial interest in one day becoming a player himself.

Greenblatt points out that the sorts of plays that Shakespeare, and any other theater-goer of the Elizabethan period, would have been exposed to primarily were morality plays, defined as "a kind of drama with personified abstract qualities as the main characters and presenting a lesson about good conduct and character." The "abstract characters" had such straightforward names as "Vice" and "Iniquity". The evidence of Shakespeare's plays demonstrates clearly that he was thoroughly exposed to the conventions of morality plays during his formative years, and he likewise capitalized on his audience's familiarity with that genre by giving his characters names that proclaimed their qualities—the meddling, ambitious Malvolio from Twelfth Night, for instance, takes his name from a portmanteau of Latin words meaning "ill will." The fact that Shakespeare did not stick exclusively to the morality play format is evidence of the "leap" that distinguishes his writing from the plays of previous centuries—where the authors of morality plays believed that useful lessons were best conveyed by boiling principles of human nature down to their essence, Shakespeare grasped that audiences were bound to be more responsive when those essential principles of humanity were attached to vibrant, recognizably human personalities.

The last, and most extraordinary, theatrical spectacle which Shakespeare may have been witness to in his childhood was Elizabeth I's fantastical "progress" to Kenilworth. Elizabeth made a habit of theses progresses, slow journeys across England along main roads in which she rode in plain view of the public. She believed that the best way to keep her throne secure was to gain the love of the common people—and that the best way to gain that love was to let the common people have a glimpse of her whenever convenient. Elizabeth presented herself for inspection more often than any British monarch before her, accepting speeches and gifts and tokens from such an array of her subjects that her Spanish ambassador felt she was forsaking the detachment and dignity that befit a queen.

In 1575, when William Shakespeare was eleven years old, Elizabeth made the most lavish progress of her reign, a fifteen-day journey to the home of her courtier and would-be suitor, Robert Dudley. Since her ascension in 1559, Dudley had been attempting to persuade the queen to marry him, and this progress to his home in Warwickshire was undertaken at his expense, in a last-ditch effort to press his suit. It would have looked something like a parade to Shakespeare, at once solemn, sacred, and festive. Elizabeth had a remarkable talent for spectacle, and these progresses were a chance to display the wealth and power of the English throne and its occupant to all who gazed upon them. The ordinary folk of Stratford would have seen nothing else like it in their lifetimes. For a sensitive, observant playwright in the making, such as the eleven year old Shakespeare, it would have been sufficient to supply him with a lifetime's worth of glorious imagery, which was at his service when he created characters such as Titania, the faerie queen from *Midsummer Night's Dream,* and Cleopatra from *Antony and Cleopatra.*

According to *Some Observations Upon the Life, &etc., of Mr. William Shakespear,* Nicholas Rowe's early biographical sketch, Shakespeare's education ended when his father fell into financial difficulties and was forced to withdraw him from the school when he was thirteen. Whether or not this was actually the case admits of some dispute; Rowe's biographical essay is notoriously full of errors. What is certain is that the next verifiable event in Shakespeare's life was his marriage, at the age of eighteen, to Anne Hathaway, age twenty-six.

Chapter Two: The Lost Years: 1578-1582

What did Shakespeare do after finishing school?

The periods from 1578 to 1582, and then again from 1585 to 1592, are known as Shakespeare's "lost years", because we have no verifiable intelligence as to what might have been occurring in Shakespeare's life then. In 1578, his father John fell behind in his taxes; this is around the time that Rowe supposes Shakespeare must have been forced to leave school. If he did leave school, we do not know what else he was doing to pass the time until four years later, in 1582, when Shakespeare was married. His three children were born between 1583 and 1585, and Shakespeare again disappears from the historical record from the time that his wife gave birth to twins until he was found in London seven years later, an actor, playwright, and part-owner of a theatrical company.

The following excerpt from *Some Observations Upon the Life* contains Nicholas Rowe's attempts to account for Shakespeare's movements after his marriage, before he came to London:

"Upon [Shakespeare's] leaving school, he seems to have given intirely into that way of living which his father propos'd to him; and in order to settle in the world after a family manner, he thought fit to marry while he was yet very young. His wife was the daughter of one Hathaway, said to have been a substantial yeoman in the neighbourhood of Stratford.

"In this kind of settlement he continu'd for some time, 'till an extravagance that he was guilty of forc'd him both out of his country and that way of living which he had taken up; and tho' it seem'd at first to be a blemish upon his good manners, and a misfortune to him, yet it afterwards happily prov'd the occasion of exerting one of the greatest Genius's that ever was known in dramatick Poetry. He had, by a misfortune common enough to young fellows, fallen into ill company; and amongst them, some that made a frequent practice of Deer-stealing, engag'd him with them more than once in robbing a Park that belong'd to Sir Thomas Lucy of Cherlecot near Stratford. For this he was prosecuted by that gentleman, as he thought, somewhat too severely; and in order to revenge that ill usage, he made a ballad upon him. And tho' this, probably the first essay of his Poetry, be lost, yet it is said to have been so very bitter, that it redoubled the prosecution against him to that degree, that he was oblig'd to leave his business and family in Warwickshire, for some time, and shelter himself in London.

"It is at this time, and upon this accident, that he is said to have made his first acquaintance in the Play-house. He was receiv'd into the Company then in being, at first in a very mean rank; but his admirable wit, and the natural turn of it to the stage, soon distinguish'd him, if not as an extraordinary Actor, yet as an excellent Writer. His name is printed, as the custom was in those times, amongst those of the other Players, before some old Plays, but without any particular account of what sort of parts he us'd to play; and tho' I have inquir'd, I could never meet with any further account of him this way, than that the top of his Performance was the Ghost in his own Hamlet. I should have been much more pleas'd to have learn'd from some certain authority, which was the first Play he wrote; it would be without doubt a pleasure to any man, curious in things of this kind, to see and know what was the first essay of a fancy like Shakespear's. Perhaps we are not to look for his beginnings, like those of other authors, among their least perfect writings; art had so little, and nature so large a share in what he did, that, for ought I know, the performances of his youth, as they were the most vigorous, and had the most fire and strength of imagination in 'em, were the best."

     We have no idea whether any of this is true—whether or not Shakespeare actually poached a deer from Sir Thomas Lucy's park, or whether his leaving Stratford for London was at all motivated by a wish to escape the backlash of having written an insulting song about Lucy that entered popular folklore. Such songs certainly existed. One story claims that Rowe was able to find an elderly woman living near Shakespeare's birthplace who was able to sing him two stanzas of a ballad about Lucy, for which Rowe paid her the price of a new gown. The song which she sang for him implied that Lucy was wasting his time, worrying about the horned deer in his park, while his wife was busily supplying him with cuckold's horns to wear at home. Another, equally unflattering song about Lucy is now popularly attributed to Shakespeare, and it appears below:

"A parliamente member, a justice of the peace,
At home a poore scarecrow, at London an asse.
If lowsie is Lucy, as some volke miscalle it,
Then Lucy is lowsie whatever befalle it:

He thinkes himselfe greate,
Yet an asse in his state,
We allowe by his eares but with asses to mate.
If Lucy is lowsie, as some volke miscalle it,
Sing lowsie Lucy, whatever befalle it."

It cannot be known whether these verses are indeed one of Shakespeare's earliest surviving compositions, though they are certainly scathing, and it is satisfying to imagine that, even as a teenager, Shakespeare was capable of savaging his enemies by writing verses that would live on in popular memory.

As to what Shakespeare was doing during the earlier period for which we have no records, between his leaving school and his marriage, it can only be conjectured that he worked. His family was not wealthy enough, especially after his father's tax difficulties, for their oldest son to idle the days away, even to practice writing. Since his father was a glover and dealer in leather goods, it would make sense to suppose that Shakespeare worked in his shop, selling gloves. Greenblatt notes that a pair of gloves purchased from John Shakespeare's shop in 1582 reached its recipient accompanied by an unasked-for short poem scribbled on a slip of paper: "The gift is small, the will is all. / Alexander Aspinall." (Aspinall was the name of the purchaser.) The woman who received the gloves as a gift retained the scrap of poetry, and told people in later years that it was the work of the famous poet Shakespeare. While this cannot be verified, it is easy to imagine how a young man with a clever, active mind and a bent towards wordplay would grow bored working in a shop, and seek to exercise his abilities by inventing the marketing jingle.

John Shakespeare's failures of fortune were such that by the time his oldest son was ready to embark on adult life, there may not have been much of a business left for him to assist with, or eventually inherit. The little we know of Shakespeare's brothers' lives contains no indication that they went into business as glovers, though they must have been able to support themselves in some line of work, because there is no record of debt, imprisonment, or any of the other pitfalls that attend a life of poverty. It would have been strange for an eldest son not to carry on his father's work, if there had been any work to carry on; forsaking his parents and the town of his birth, and leaving behind a wife and children, surely indicates that calamity of some kind befell the Shakespeare family. We can easily speculate that Shakespeare was profoundly affected in some way by his father's troubles. He was old enough that it would have been impossible for him not to notice that his father had lost the high standing he had enjoyed in Stratford when Shakespeare was a young boy, and as an adolescent he must have been acutely conscious that his family was no longer as respectable as it had once been.

Whenever Shakespeare writes about fathers, it is with a peculiar strength of feeling. The most notable example, of course, is old King Hamlet, father of the Danish prince, whose murder drives all the action of that play. *Hamlet* is notable, in part, precisely for the intensity and ambiguity of Hamlet's feelings towards a father whom he seems to have loved, feared, reverenced, and failed to relate to, all at once. When his uncle Claudius, his father's brother and murderer, attempts to console him for his father's death, his speech is so sweet and genuinely comforting that it is almost difficult to reconcile with his role as the play's villain:

"'Tis sweet and commendable in your nature, Hamlet,
To give these mourning duties to your father:
But, you must know, your father lost a father;
That father lost, lost his, and the survivor bound
In filial obligation for some term
To do obsequious sorrow: but to persever
In obstinate condolement is a course
Of impious stubbornness; 'tis unmanly grief;
It shows a will most incorrect to heaven,
A heart unfortified, a mind impatient,
An understanding simple and unschool'd:

For what we know must be and is as common
As any the most vulgar thing to sense,
Why should we in our peevish opposition
Take it to heart? Fie! 'tis a fault to heaven,
A fault against the dead, a fault to nature,
To reason most absurd: whose common theme
Is death of fathers, and who still hath cried,
From the first corse till he that died to-day,
'This must be so.' We pray you, throw to earth
This unprevailing woe, and think of us
As of a father: for let the world take note,
You are the most immediate to our throne;
And with no less nobility of love
Than that which dearest father bears his son,
Do I impart toward you.

John Shakespeare died in 1601; the closest we can come to fixing a date for Shakespeare's writing *Hamlet* is between 1599 and 1601. If the latest date is the correct one, then this speech of Claudius's was written when Shakespeare would have been in deep mourning for his father. Even if the earlier dates are more accurate, it seems apparent that Shakespeare had wrestled deeply with the idea of his father's death. Claudius, obviously, has his own motive for trying to persuade Hamlet not to dwell on the death of the man he murdered. But lines such as, "Your father lost a father, / That father lost, lost his," and "a fault against nature...whose common theme is death of fathers" are clearly the efforts of a person who has suffered a deep loss to remonstrate with himself and try to become reconciled to his grief.

Though Hamlet is driven, throughout the play, by a desire to avenge his father's death, he is notably cagey on the subject of his feelings about his father. In the same scene, after Claudius and the court have departed, Hamlet is left alone with his friend Horatio, where he speaks of his father in a personal way for the first and only time in the play:

> HAMLET
> My father!--methinks I see my father.
>
> HORATIO
> Where, my lord?
>
> HAMLET
> In my mind's eye, Horatio.
>
> HORATIO
> I saw him once; he was a goodly king.
>
> HAMLET
> He was a man, take him for all in all,
> I shall not look upon his like again.

Hamlet's epitaph on his father is remarkably free of praise, awe, or sentimentality. It is as if he cannot find words sufficient to encapsulate the huge personality of the warlike king who must have dominated the worldview of his peculiar, scholarly son. "He was a man, take him for all in all," seems to encompass and forgive a host of faults; "I shall not look upon his like again" calls to mind the high standing that John Shakespeare once held in Stratford, his involvement in so many different important civic offices, the great abilities and winning personality that must have endeared him to his countrymen and made him such a trusted member of the community. Though we cannot be certain what drove William Shakespeare from Stratford to London, it seems evident that the domestic drama of his father's fall from grace must have played some role in it.

Theories

What Shakespeare did between the end of his education and his marriage to Anne Hathaway has been hotly debated for centuries. It seems certain that he worked in his father's shop for a time, and equally certain that he did not do so for long. Past this, the only evidence for what occupations he might have pursued are based on clues found in his plays. Scholars have speculated that, based on his accurate use of legal terminology, he might have worked as a clerk in a lawyer's office, a position his grammar school education would have made him eligible for. Another theory posits that he joined the Earl of Leicester's military campaign to defend Protestants in the Netherlands against the Spanish, because he makes equally deft usage of military terms. It has even been suggested that he boarded a ship bound for North America on one of Walter Raleigh's voyages to Virginia—the idea of the New World clearly fascinated Shakespeare, as evidenced by plays such as *The Tempest*.

However, we must consider that it is unlikely that he could have done all of these things—and yet, the plays reflect knowledge of all these vocations. We can explain this by taking the anti-Stratfordian view, and assuming that someone with a much better education and wider experience of the world wrote the plays (or that they were written as a collaboration between several people who encompassed all these experiences between them). Or we can explain it by referring to the one fact about Shakespeare that admits of no doubt whatsoever: that he was extraordinarily adept at language, to the point that he delighted in making bilingual puns, and could absorb the trade-specific terminology of any profession and use jargon as if he had intimate personal knowledge of it. The latter explanation is the simplest, but it gets us no closer to devising a plausible theory as to what Shakespeare was doing during his "lost years".

Another theory, a somewhat vague one, supposes that he must have been doing something that enabled him to acquire all the skills that an Elizabethan actor, or player, would have to have possessed. Considering that actors were legally classified as "vagabaonds", virtually without legal status and liable to being treated with even less dignity than a servant, they had to be fairly well-rounded individuals, able to pass themselves off as kings and noblemen. They had to look good in a suit of fine clothes, be excellent dancers and competent musicians, and mimic refined manners and speech. The most straightforward means of acquiring these skills was apprenticeship, but even though Shakespeare would have been about the right age to become a player's apprentice during his first "lost" period of life, it is unlikely that he was one. We know this because he got married when he was eighteen. If he had been an apprentice, his term of service would still have been ongoing in his late teens, and he would not have been permitted to marry. That he did marry, and proceed to produce a family in short order, is one of the few things we know about him without any doubt.

Shakespeare and religion

Another theory regarding Shakespeare's activities prior to his marriage is that he was employed for a few years as a schoolmaster by a wealthy Catholic gentleman in the north of England. This suggestion comes from a fairly reliable source: it was told to the 17th century writer John Aubrey by the son of a man who had been one of Shakespeare's colleagues and fellow players. If this is true, it opens up serious speculation as to what Shakespeare's private religious feelings might have been, owing to the political climate of the time. It was necessary, during the reign of Elizabeth I, to be "conforming"—that is, to attend Anglican church services and to eschew any outward loyalty to Catholic beliefs and practices—if one wanted to avoid imprisonment, let alone be employed in most jobs.

John Shakespeare was certainly a scrupulous conformist; as an alderman in Stratford, he had been responsible for ordering the destruction of all the old Catholic paintings of saints and martyrs at the local guild hall. But the Protestant Reformation was at that time so recent that virtually every family had members who adhered to the old Catholic beliefs, at least in the privacy of their own conscience, and it wasn't uncommon for individuals to feel deep conflict as well. An entire generation of people who had been educated as faithful Catholics in childhood were required, by royal decree, to throw off the trappings of Rome seemingly overnight; the transition was often anything but seamless. John Shakespeare could not have risked bringing his children up as anything but outwardly conforming Protestants. But there is the matter of his recusancy to take into consideration; many Catholics took on the liability of the fines for non-attendance at church rather than compromise their beliefs.

Even if John Shakespeare had no religious ambiguities to pass on to William, the schoolmaster who was employed at the Stratford grammar school when Shakespeare was a student did. Simon Hunt left Stratford when Shakespeare was eleven, and he left England to join the French Catholic seminary at Douai, a choice which must have reflected the deepest promptings of his conscience. Seminaries in Europe were, at that time, training priests for "the English mission"; for most priests, this meant nothing more sinister than celebrating the mass in private homes and hearing the confession of English Catholics in secret, but a small number of priests were dispatched to raise a rebellion against Elizabeth in preparation for the planned invasion of the Spanish Armada. Hunt would have known that he could never return to England openly; he would be arrested as soon as he set foot on English soil. His religious sentiments must have stolen into his schoolroom lessons to a certain degree, because when Hunt left England he took one of his students with him, a boy some seven years older than Shakespeare.

If Simon Hunt singled out the young William Shakespeare as one of the few pupils whose religious conscience he could hope to shape, he had good reason for doing so. Shakespeare's mother's family, the Ardens, were known to be Catholic; it is possible that Mary Shakespeare passed her beliefs on to her oldest son, or at the very least, it is possible that Hunt assumed that she did, and set out to reinforce those beliefs. Paranoia about Catholics plotting and saying Masses in secret was so extensive that sometimes the houses of suspected Catholics were searched by the Queen's armed guards. Stephen Greenblatt theorizes that:

"...if William's mother, Mary, was a pious Catholic, like her father, she may have kept religious tokens—a rosary, a medal, a crucifix... And if the searchers had done a thorough job...they might have found a highly compromising document to which John Shakespeare had apparently set his name: a piously Catholic 'spiritual testament,' belying his public adherence to the Reformed faith."

The "spiritual testament" signed by John Shakespeare was found in the 1700's when a house which had once belonged to his family was demolished. There are some doubts as to its authenticity, but the story is a suggestive one, if only because John Shakespeare played a role in hiring Simon Hunt to teach at his son's school, and because of Mary Shakespeare's known ties to staunch Catholics.

It is difficult to read the plays of William Shakespeare and come away with any sense that the author was a deeply pious person, committed heart and soul to one particular religious creed. If Shakespeare's parents—mother, father, or both—were indeed secretly Catholic, it is mostly relevant on two points. The first is that a sensitive, clever, feeling child must have been strongly affected by the sense of secrecy and peril that would have attended the practice of forbidden religious ceremonies by his family. He would undoubtedly have gained the impression that it is worth risking any degree of danger or pain to one's physical body in order to save the soul—and the battle for the soul is a dramatic recurring theme in Shakespeare's writing. The second is that, if Shakespeare was ever permitted to witness the gorgeous, elaborate trappings of an old-fashioned Catholic mass, it might well have been the experience which first taught him the power of theatrical spectacles.

Reading Shakespeare, it is evident that his imagination was not immune to being played upon by visions of dark, mysterious forces at work in the universe—witchcraft, prophecies, miracles, etc.—or to the consolation of Christian doctrine, which holds that the soul is eternal, and virtue is rewarded, in the afterlife if not sooner. But his imagination was not confined by the boundaries of theology. Shakespeare's most virtuous characters, like Marina, the lost princess from *Pericles,* are not merely pious; their virtue appears as some kind of luminous inborn characteristic, possessing a power that does not necessarily stem from a preoccupation with godly matters, though it evokes Christian imagery. Likewise, his most villainous characters, like Iago, are spurred on by the perverse promptings of their own minds, not by compacts with demons and devils. Even Macbeth, so famous for consorting with witches, does not murder Duncan because the witches have placed a spell on him—he is ensorcelled by his own imagination, acting on nothing more than suggestion.

Aldous Huxley, the famous 20th century author of *Brave New World,* which takes its title from *The Tempest,* speculated about Shakespeare's religious beliefs in an essay written just before his death in 1964:

"Religion is not merely a complex of behavior-patterns and organizations. It is also a set of beliefs. What were Shakespeare's beliefs? The question is not an easy one to answer; for in the first place Shakespeare was a dramatist who made his characters express opinions which were appropriate to them, but which may not have been those of the poet. And anyhow did he himself have the same beliefs, without alteration or change or emphasis, throughout his life?

"The poet's basic Christianity is very beautifully expressed in Measure for Measure, where the genuinely saintly Isabella reminds Angelo, the self-righteous Pillar of Society, of the divine scheme of redemption and of the ethical consequences which ought to flow from its acceptance as an article of faith-ought to flow but, alas, generally do not flow!

> Alas, alas!
> Why, all the souls that were forfeit once;
> and He that might the vantage best have took
> found out the remedy. How would you be,
> if He, which is the top of judgement, should
> but judge you as you are? O, think on that;
> and mercy then will breathe within your lips,
> like man new-made.

"These lines, I would say, express very clearly the essence of Shakespeare's Christianity. But the essence of Christianity can assume a wide variety of denominational forms. The Reverend Richard Davies, a clergyman who flourished toward the end of the seventeenth century, declared categorically that Shakespeare had "died a papist." There is no corroborative evidence of this, and it seems on the face of it unlikely; but almost anything is possible, especially on a death-bed. What is certain is that Shakespeare did not live a papist; for, if he had, he would have found himself in chronic and serious trouble with the law, and vehemently suspected of treason.... (The casuists of the Roman curia had let it be known that the assassination of the heretic Queen Elizabeth would not be a sin; on the contrary, it would be registered in the murderer's credit column as a merit.) There is, therefore, every reason to suppose that Shakespeare lived a member of the Church of England. However, the theology which finds expression in his plays is by no means consistently Protestant. Purgatory has no place in the Protestant world-picture, but in Hamlet and in Measure for Measure the existence of Purgatory is taken for granted.

"'I am thy father's spirit,' says the Ghost to Hamlet,
'doom'd for a certain term to walk the night,
and for the day confin'd to fast in fires,
till the foul crimes done in my days of nature
are burnt and purg'd away. But that I am forbid
to tell the secrets of my prison-house,
I could a tale unfold, whose lightest word
would harrow up thy soul;
freeze thy young blood;
make thy two eyes, like stars, start
from their spheres....

"And men are capable of greater wickedness even than women. "Use every man after his desert, and who would 'scape whipping?" There is, no doubt, some kind of moral order. The good go to Heaven, the evil to Purgatory and Hell. And even here on earth it can sometimes be observed that "the gods are just and of our pleasant vices make instruments to plague us." But divine justice is tempered by divine malignity. "As flies to wanton boys are we to the gods-they kill us for their sport." And to the effects of divine malignity must be added those of man's wickedness and stupidity, and the workings of a blind fate completely indifferent to human ideals and values. Sickness, decrepitude, death lie in wait for everyone."

Chapter Three: From Stratford to London

"Most couples, [Shakespeare] may have told himself, are mismatched, even couples marrying for love; you should never marry in haste; a young man should not marry an older woman; a marriage under compulsion—'wedlock forced'—is a hell. And perhaps, beyond these, he told himself, in imagining Hamlet and Macbeth, Othello, and The Winter's Tale, that marital intimacy is dangerous, that the very dream is a threat."

Stephen Greenblatt, *Will in the World*

Marriage

The information we possess regarding Shakespeare's marriage casts a mysterious pall over the event. On the 27th of November, 1582, the Worcester church register recorded that a marriage license had been granted to two persons by the names of "Wm Shaxpere" and "Annam Whateley." Then, on the following day, November 28th, the following entry appears in the parish register:

"Noverint universi per praesentes nos Fulconem Sandells de Stratford in comitatu Warwici agricolam et Johannem Rychardson ibidem agricolam, teneri et firmiter obligari Ricardo Cosin generoso et Roberto Warmstry notario publico in quadraginta libris bonae et legalis monetae Angliae solvend. eisdem Ricardoet Roberto haered. execut. et assignat. suis ad quam quidem solucionem bene et fideliter faciend. obligamus nos et utrumque nostrum per se pro toto et in solid. haered. executor. et administrator. nostros firmiter per praesentes sigillis nostris sigillat. Dat. 28 die Novem. Anno regni dominae nostrae Eliz. Dei gratia Angliae Franc. et Hiberniae Reginae fidei defensor &c.25.2 The condition of this obligation is such that if hereafter there shall not appear any lawful let or impediment by reason of any precontract, consanguinity, affinity or by any other lawful means whatsoever, but that William Shagspere on the one party and Anne Hathwey of Stratford in the diocese of Worcester, maiden, may lawfully solemnize matrimony together, and in the same afterwards remain and continue like man and wife according unto the laws in that behalf provided..."

William Shakespeare was thus married to Anne Hathaway. Scholars have debated for centuries whether "Annam Whateley" and "Anne Hathwey" were the same person, and if not, what could have happened to change Shakespeare's plans so drastically as to make him seek a marriage with one woman on November 27, only to marry a different woman on November 28.

Anne Hathaway was in an unusual position for a young woman of her era. In Elizabethan England, and unmarried woman was bound in obedience to her family, by custom if not by law, long after she reached the age of majority at 21. She would not have been able to earn an independent living; even if she obtained a job as a servant, she would then be dependent on the family she worked for. But Hathaway was an orphan, and her father had left her a small property—this did not make her rich, but it made her self-sufficient, and most importantly, it meant that she did not have to answer to anyone for her comings and goings, or for the company she kept. A young man who wished to court a young woman typically had to win the favor not only of his prospective bride, but of her family; but a young man interested in courting Anne Hathaway had only to persuade her, and this, it can be surmised, would have been attractive to many men in Stratford.

"Annam Whateley" and Anne Hathaway may well have been the same person. Spelling, in 16th century England, was recklessly irregular. It was not uncommon for legal documents to be signed with "marks", if the person was illiterate, and those who could write their names often changed the spelling from one occasion to the next. Furthermore, the clerk who was in charge of drawing up the marriage licenses in the Worcester church was notorious for writing names down wrong; there is documentation to prove that he made other errors in the recording of names that fell even further from the mark than writing "Whateley" for "Hathaway". ("Annam" was probably just a poor attempt at Latinizing "Anne".)

The suggestion that Shakespeare might have been in love with one woman whom he abandoned for another has fired the imaginations of scholars for centuries, for two principle reasons: Hathaway was six years older than Shakespeare, and she was probably pregnant at the time of their marriage, because their first child was baptized six months after the wedding took place. Since there would have been considerable pressure on the couple to marry in the event of a pregnancy, it is easy to see why so many people have spun a story of resentment, forced marriage, and domestic unhappiness around Shakespeare's union with Anne Hathaway—and the dramatic dimensions of the story only get juicier if one supposes that Shakespeare's true affections lay with another woman. But as with so many other aspects of Shakespeare's biography, the popular narrative of his unwilling marriage is founded on coincidences that can be explained another way. For instance, Hathaway might not have been pregnant when they married; Susanna Shakespeare, born in May of 1583, might simply have been a premature baby. Or, even if Hathaway was pregnant, she might have been only a month or so along, rather than fully three months pregnant and showing, which might have made the marriage a matter of urgency.

The Elizabethan era was not quite so Puritanical as the Victorian era. It was irregular, but not terribly uncommon for women to be pregnant when they were married. So long as there was an "understanding" between the couple, and the marriage took place in time for the child to escape the stigma of bastardry, society generally turned a blind eye if the baby was born sooner than a full nine months after the wedding. Probably the strongest argument for the marriage having been motivated by a pregnancy is based on Shakespeare's age. Eighteen was considered quite young to be married, even in the 16th century; then, as now, it was more usual for men of the lower classes to marry in their late twenties, once they had amassed some money and had a home of their own. Anne Hathaway was not, as some biographers have insisted, an old maid whose chances at matrimony were diminishing; twenty-six was a normal age for marriage, and her independent financial situation would have made her an eligible prospect for as long as she was of child-bearing age, and perhaps after. Shakespeare's age does suggest, however, that there was no second, scorned woman by the name of Whateley in his life. He would have had no good reason for seeking a marriage to any woman, however much he loved her, before he had enough money to support them both, unless there was some pressing reason to hasten their union.

Shakespeare's marriage to Hathaway took place quickly. It was the custom, both in the Elizabethan era and for centuries afterwards, to publish "banns"—public announcements of a couple's intention to marry—for three weeks prior to the service taking place. This allowed ample opportunity for people in the community to come forward with objections to the match, if they had any, such as knowledge of a prior marriage, information that reflected poorly on someone's character. It was also an opportunity for the family of the bride or groom to forbid the wedding from taking place. In Shakespeare's case, any objection on the part of his family could have derailed his plans, because he was still, technically, a minor. But the usual three-week waiting period was waved for Shakespeare and Hathaway. This was effected through perfectly legal means; two local businessmen who had been friends with Hathaway's father offered up a bond of forty pounds to speed the marriage along. If the wedding had taken place in secret, without the knowledge of Shakespeare's family, the fact that the banns had been waived meant that they could have sued for the marriage to be annulled, in which case the forty pound bond would be used to pay for the court case. But no such objection or attempted annulment seems to have been offered, and Hathaway's father's friends were allowed to keep their money.

Six months after the marriage, Shakespeare's eldest child, Susanna, was born in May of 1583. Two years later, Anne Hathaway Shakespeare gave births to twins, Judith and Hamnet, in 1585. From 1585 until 1592, when Shakespeare first surfaces in London, we have no knowledge of his activities or whereabouts. There is no record of any correspondence between Shakespeare and Hathaway, which suggests she probably could not read or write. Biographers have also interpreted the physical distance between them as a sign that Shakespeare had never wanted the marriage in the first place, and relished his freedom and bachelor lifestyle in London. For this, as for every other conjecture made about Shakespeare's life, scholars have divined the existence of evidence in the texts of his plays and poems.

The first record of Shakespeare after the birth of his twin children is connected to the first performances of *2 Henry VI,* in March of 1592. Shortly afterwards, in 1593, he published the long romantic poem *"Venus and Adonis"*. In this poem, a fair and lovely young man is pursued and courted by an "older woman"—that is, an immortal goddess. The opening stanzas depict the goddess sick with love for the mortal youth, chasing after him with a boldness and lack of reserve that stand in stark contrast to the typical model of the passionate male wooer attempting to overcome the chaste aloofness of his girlish beloved:

EVEN as the sun with purple-colour'd face
Had ta'en his last leave of the weeping morn,
Rose-cheek'd Adonis hied him to the chase;
Hunting he loved, but love he laugh'd to scorn;
Sick-thoughted Venus makes amain unto him,
And like a bold-faced suitor 'gins to woo him.

'Thrice-fairer than myself,' thus she began,
'The field's chief flower, sweet above compare,

Stain to all nymphs, more lovely than a man,
More white and red than doves or roses are;
Nature that made thee, with herself at strife,
Saith that the world hath ending with thy life.

'Vouchsafe, thou wonder, to alight thy steed,
And rein his proud head to the saddle-bow;
If thou wilt deign this favour, for thy meed
A thousand honey secrets shalt thou know:
Here come and sit, where never serpent hisses,
And being set, I'll smother thee with kisses;

'And yet not cloy thy lips with loathed satiety,
But rather famish them amid their plenty,
Making them red and pale with fresh variety,
Ten kisses short as one, one long as twenty:
A summer's day will seem an hour but short,
Being wasted in such time-beguiling sport.'

It has often been supposed that "Venus and Adonis" must represent Shakespeare's feelings about his relationship with his wife, particularly as Adonis dies without ever giving Venus the love she desires from him. In the poem, Venus is driven mad by Adonis' coyness, and her pursuit of him is nothing less than desperate:

Look how he can, she cannot choose but love;
And by her fair immortal hand she swears,
From his soft bosom never to remove,
Till he take truce with her contending tears,

Which long have rain'd, making her cheeks all wet;
And one sweet kiss shall pay this countless debt.

Upon this promise did he raise his chin,
Like a dive-dapper peering through a wave,
Who, being look'd on, ducks as quickly in;
So offers he to give what she did crave;
But when her lips were ready for his pay,
He winks, and turns his lips another way.

Never did passenger in summer's heat
More thirst for drink than she for this good turn.
Her help she sees, but help she cannot get;
She bathes in water, yet her fire must burn:
'O, pity,' 'gan she cry, 'flint-hearted boy!
'Tis but a kiss I beg; why art thou coy?'

But if one is to make inferences about Shakespeare's feelings regarding his marriage from his writing, one must also contend with the many scenes and passages in the plays which depict lovers who are eager for a hasty marriage, such as in *Romeo and Juliet,* where the entire plot centers around the lovers' mutual desire to be wed as quickly as possible, within hours of their first meeting. And there are ample examples of happily married couples in the plays, such as Coriolanus and Volumnia, his "gracious silence", who comes to visit her soldier husband after a long absence from home. There are also bitterly unhappy married couples, like

Goneril and Albany from *King Lear,* and even the Macbeths, who are somewhere in between, a husband and wife locked together in a path careening towards mutual destruction, but somehow unable to do without one another.

Greenblatt points out that Shakespeare returns often to the theme of marriages in which the wife is excluded from her husband's innermost thoughts and counsels. The Macbeths, who have sometimes been said to have the best marriage in Shakespeare, are almost unique for the profound influence that Lady Macbeth has over her husband's career ambitions. A more typical example is Portia, wife of Brutus, in Julius Caesar, who complains that she feels more like a whore than a wife because Brutus will sleep with her but not talk to her. It is worth keeping in mind that in the Elizabethan era, when people were still deeply Catholic in their attitudes towards matrimony and divorce was simply not an option for anyone of Shakespeare's class, people felt differently about marriage. Marriage was conceived of primarily as a practical necessity, to avoid the sin of fornication, solemnize the dependent state of women, generate heirs, and secure the bloodless transfer of power and property from one generation to the next. There was an inherent virtue to virginity and celibacy, in the Catholic way of thinking, and those who had the self-discipline to remain chaste all their lives were thought to be in a better condition than those who were compelled to join their fortunes with another person for life. Only when divorce became attainable to the average person did poets begin to celebrate the married state. Shakespeare, a product of his time, would have been anything but unusual if he saw marriage as a necessity along the same lines as maintaining the roof over one's head.

Still, whether or not Shakespeare resented the necessity of his marriage—if it was a necessity—and whether or not his relationship with his wife was disharmonious, it cannot be said that he put his family entirely from his mind when he left them to pursue a theatrical career in London. Hathaway probably moved into John and Mary Shakespeare's house on Henley Street when Shakespeare left Stratford in 1585, but by 1596, Shakespeare had made enough money to purchase and move his family into New Place, the largest house in town. Scholars are divided as to whether Anne and William Shakespeare functioned as long-distance business partners or whether Shakespeare made frequent journeys back to Stratford to look after his investment properties and his family. Summer was a deadly season in the large cities; disease was rampant, people died by the hundreds, and anyone who had enough money to do so fled London for the country until cooler weather returned. It would make sense for Shakespeare to have returned to Stratford once a year, since the theaters were often closed anyway. Whether he saw his wife on a regular basis or not, it is evident that he took seriously his responsibility to provide for her, and for their children.

One last piece of poetical evidence ought to be produced before conclusion is pronounced on the theoretical happiness or misery of Shakespeare's marriage to Anne Hathaway. Sonnet 145 is thought by some scholars to have been written very early in Shakespeare's career, perhaps not long after his marriage.

> Those lips that Love's own hand did make
> Breathed forth the sound that said 'I hate,'
> To me that languish'd for her sake:
> But when she saw my woeful state,
> Straight in her heart did mercy come,
> Chiding that tongue that ever sweet
> Was used in giving gentle doom,
> And taught it thus anew to greet:
> 'I hate' she alter'd with an end,
> That follow'd it as gentle day
> Doth follow night, who like a fiend
> From heaven to hell is flown away;

> 'I hate' from hate away she threw,
> And saved my life, saying -- 'not you.'

The phrase in the sonnet's concluding couplet, "hate away", has been conjectured to be a play on the name "Hathaway". It is neither more nor less compelling than any other conjecture made about Shakespeare based on the evidence of his writing, but if one prefers to imagine that Shakespeare experienced some degree of happiness with his chosen partner in life, then it is comforting to imagine that at least one of his brilliant love poems was written with Anne Hathaway in mind.

When Shakespeare died, he left almost the entirety of his by now considerable wealth and property to his older daughter, Susanna, and made her and her husband the executors of his estate. He had retired from the stage to live in Stratford full-time, and it may be significant that he moved into New Place with his wife, rather than living apart from her in one of his other properties. But then there is the matter of Anne Shakespeare's inheritance. Shakespeare's will is elaborately detailed, as he was, by the end of his life, a successful businessman, and though it makes provisions for friends, siblings, and both his surviving children, it mentions Anne only once, in an addendum to the first draft of the document: "Item: I give unto my wife my second best bed with the furniture." It is difficult to put a sentimental spin on this, or to interpret it as a gesture of love. But widows were entitled to one-third of their husband's estate while they lived, so Anne Shakespeare was probably already well provided for; there is no reason to suppose that her daughter Susanna would have failed to share her large inheritance with her mother. Some scholars have wondered if there was some private joke shared between Shakespeare and Hathaway to which the second-best bed was the punchline. There seems little other potential for sentimentality in the gesture. If Shakespeare loved his wife, it nonetheless seems that by the end of his life he had absolved himself of responsibility for her.

Shakespeare leaves Stratford

It is not known why Shakespeare left behind his parents, siblings, wife, and three young children, when, precisely, he left, or where he may have gone at first. We lose track of him in 1585, after the twins Judith and Hamnet were born, and though he resurfaces in London in 1592, it does not necessarily follow that he went directly there.

Nicholas Rowe, as we discussed in an earlier chapter, holds that Shakespeare was forced to flee the area—"the country", in the Elizabethan way of speaking—because he fell in with bad company and was caught poaching a deer in Sir Thomas Lucy's park, and afterwards incited that gentleman to prosecute him to the fullest extent of the law by writing a rude song about him which became so popular as to outlive both its author and its object of ridicule. This tale is no longer considered as plausible as it once was, but if true, it is interesting. Deer-poaching in Shakespeare's time was much less often the desperate act of a starving man hunting for his dinner, and more often the act of a thrill-seeking Oxford undergraduate acting on a dare or a bet. And all the versions of the story that Rowe tells (there were at least four, from different sources) had one thing in common: that Shakespeare's rude song was written in retaliation for having received a harsher punishment than was usual, or even legal, for poachers caught in the act. There is a suggestion in some accounts that he was whipped, which was not merely very painful, but would have been deeply humiliating for the son of a respectable, prosperous man, newly married and a father.

The poaching story, whether it is true or not, is at the very least considered a satisfying explanation for Shakespeare's sudden departure from his home town, because no matter how talented he was—and obviously, history has concluded that no one has been more talented—it is highly unlikely that he decided one day to simply leave behind his network of well-established family connections and make his fortunes by his pen in London. The Romantic image of the starving artist toiling away at his poetry in a garret in the big city was not present in the Elizabethan consciousness. Society's stratifications had not yet been so broken down by the emergence of the middle class as to permit such a fancy to take hold in the mind of a fairly well-off young man who must have known that he was trading comfort and security for risk, hard work, and virtually no promise of reward. Something serious undoubtedly happened to send the young William Shakespeare to London, and the simplest explanation is that he was in some sort of legal trouble.

Another possible explanation is that Shakespeare himself first circulated the poaching story as a cover for some far more serious legal difficulty. Sir Thomas Lucy was a noted hunter of recusants. If Shakespeare's family was suspected in their Catholic sympathies, and especially if Shakespeare did travel north to become a schoolmaster in a Catholic family before his marriage, any rumor or hint of his having gotten into legal difficulties because of Lucy might spell disaster for him if it reached London.

By spinning a yarn involving youthful hijinks, daring acts of trespass on forbidden lands, and a comical ending, Shakespeare might have effectively explained away any troubling rumors that depicted him as the rightful target of a famous persecutor of Catholics. Warwickshire, of which Stratford is a part, was a virtual hotbed of seditious Catholic activity in the 1580's, and Shakespeare would have been under a partial cloud of suspicion simply by virtue of having come from there. Furthermore, Sir Thomas Lucy played a role in the apprehension of John Somerville, a young nobleman from a Catholic family who was arrested for treason after he proclaimed publicly that he intended to assassinate Queen Elizabeth. Somerville was married to the daughter of Edward Arden, who was related to the same Arden family to which Mary Shakespeare belonged. John Somerville and William Shakespeare may have been distant cousins; they may even have known each other. Whether or not the connection was a personal one for Shakespeare, he undoubtedly knew of Somerville's fate; it became common knowledge, especially in London, after he and his father were decapitated and their heads displayed on pikes.

Robert Dudley, Earl of Leicester and lifelong friend, favorite, and advisor to the Queen, was one of the most militant, puritanical Protestants in England, and Sir Thomas Lucy was one of his chief deputies; it was from Leicester that Lucy received his knighthood. After Edward Arden was arrested, Lucy made it his special purpose to investigate all of the Arden family connections, believing that Somerville's actions bespoke a deep-seated conspiracy that involved all his relations. Even if Shakespeare was not personally acquainted with Somerville or that branch of the Arden family, Lucy was certainly acquainted with Shakespeare and his father, and thus would have known of their family connection. This alone might have made Shakespeare uneasy enough to leave the seat of so much unrest behind and seek his fortune elsewhere. London was a hard place to make a living, but it had one inarguable virtue: a solitary man could be anonymous there as he could be in few other places in England. He might have set out for London on his own with the intention of seeking out a theatrical career. Or, what is even more likely, he might have encountered a traveling troupe of players who were touring Warwickshire at the time, and decided to throw his lot in with them.

London

At the time of Shakespeare's arrival in London—whether that arrival was in 1585, directly after the birth of his twin children, or whether it was closer to his appearance in the theater in 1592—theaters, as we understand them, were very new inventions. Play-acting was an ancient art, of course, but England had no playhouses dedicated solely to theatrical performances until Elizabeth's reign. Theaters flourished during the long period of political stability and steady economic growth of the Elizabethan era, so that by the time Shakespeare appeared to make his mark on the theatrical world, there were several highly competitive companies of players for him to choose between, assuming his loyalties were not already committed to whichever company had helped him escape Stratford. Elizabeth I was extremely fond of plays, which helped to confer a degree of legitimacy on the players themselves, but playhouses, on the other hand, were considered by many to be only half a step above whorehouses.

This was partly because the various kinds of popular entertainment that were found in London in the late 16th century tended to mingle together in one huge open spectacle in evenings.

The earliest theaters were inn-yards, that is, the cobbled courtyards in front of taverns, which provided ready access to refreshment in the form of alcohol. It was normal for plays to be preceded by bear-baitings, a particularly cruel yet immensely popular form of entertainment in which old, feeble, blind bears were tied to stakes and attacked by dogs; other animals, like monkeys and apes, were also induced to fight wild dogs for the benefit of audiences. If it is difficult to imagine how anyone would have had the stomach to watch such a bloody spectacle of animal cruelty, yet alone eagerly seek out such events on a nightly basis, it must be considered in the context of another sort of spectacle that was common for the average Londoner to witness: the public punishment of criminals. Executions—beheadings for the high-born, hangings for the lower classes—were conducted before avid crowds, to say nothing of the whippings, maimings, and long periods of being confined in stocks that were doled out as punishment for lesser offenses. Even someone like Shakespeare, a newcomer from a country town, would have been accustomed to seeing corporal sentences carried out in public, though with nowhere near the frequency that they happened in London.

Besides the drinking, the bear-baitings, the gambling that took place around the bear-baitings, the professional sex workers scouting the crowds for customers, the low social status of the players themselves, and the hint of illicit homosexuality and cross-dressing that attended every love scene performed between two male actors, there was the very real danger which the theaters (and every other spectacle which drew a crowd to a confined space) posed as a breeding-ground for disease. Bubonic plague, cholera, typhus, and a mysterious and as-yet-unidentified illness known as the "sweating sickness" killed more people in London every year than were born. It is not so difficult, therefore, to understand why the theaters were so often condemned by city officials as a public menace.

Though plays were just as popular amongst the wealthy and upper classes as they were amongst the poor, the gentry and the nobles did not have to attend the theater to see the plays if they did not want to. They had the luxury of hiring the players for private performances given in the galleries and halls of their own houses, for the entertainment of themselves, their families, and their guests. In Elizabethan England, everyone worked for someone else; everyone had a master. A masterless man or woman had no protection in the eyes of the law and were subject to punishments reserved for the very lowest members of society. Acting troupes, therefore, had to have noble patrons for their own protection, which is why all the theatrical societies of Shakespeare's day were known by names such as the King's Men, or the Lord Chamberlain's men. But even though they depended on the patronage of the nobility in order to continue existing, they made the bulk of their money by filling the playhouses with far less respectable customers.

This dichotomy created a peculiar sort of tension in the actor's life. He had to look and sound the part of a gentleman, even a lord or a king, in his speech and dress, be able to dance well and play musical instruments; in short, in order to play his roles, he had to acquire all of the outward characteristics that set the wealthy apart from the baseborn. But legally and socially, he was considered little better than a vagrant. He had to flatter and court noble patrons, even though the better part of his livelihood depended on his ability to appeal to uneducated, unrefined theater-goers. And for Shakespeare, who was writing plays as well as acting in them, there was an additional risk involved; he must entertain without being offensive, lest the content of his plays anger the public censors. Plays were banned on all sorts of pretexts, and having a play banned was a serious financial setback for a company of players.

Throughout Shakespeare's plays, authority takes on various guises, running the gamut from the honest, stupid Dogberry of Much Ado About Nothing, to the brilliant, sinister Angelo of Measure for Measure. Shakespeare clearly had the ability to stake out a lucrative career in the Elizabethan theater, a career rewarded with financial success and, eventually, upward social mobility, which indicates that he must have had a special knack for playing the game—keeping powerful people on the right side of him, inviting audiences to laugh at aristocratic characters without crossing the line and giving too much offense. But part of his artistic success lies in his ability to subtly critique those in power. Shakespeare's attitude towards authority is not based on anachronistic notions of the dignity of the common man, or the rights of the lower classes—such ideas did not become popular in Europe until the Enlightenment in the 18th century. But his portrayal of sheriffs, constables, judges, lords, and kings displays an intelligent, feeling person's cutting observations on the hypocrisy and injustice often found in those who hold the power in a rigidly hierarchical society, as well as extended meditations on the nature of mercy.

In Dogberry, we find a country constable who possesses the necessary authority to arrest Conrad, the servant of the villainous Prince John, when he overhears Conrad conspiring to slander Hero and prevent her marriage to Claudio. But as the servant of a prince, Conrad ranks higher in the social order than Dogberry does, which makes his arrest nothing less than an utter humiliation. Shakespeare's audience must have relished this humiliation, because it is no more than Conrad deserves for his role in ruining Hero's reputation. But they must also have been gratified by the fact that there were very few occasions when the lowborn had the opportunity to serve justice on those above them. Indeed, Shakespeare takes care to point out that the only way Dogberry managed it was by accident. Conrad is so incensed by the role reversal involved in Dogberry's having authority over him that he loses his temper and calls him an ass. Dogberry responds with a monologue that is at once comical, because of his habit of mistaking the meanings of words, and poignant, because it so clearly touches on a subject about which he feels deeply—namely, his hard-won respectability and his claims to status in the community:

> Dost thou not suspect my place? dost thou not suspect my years? O that he were here to write me down an ass! But, masters, remember that I am an ass; though it be not written down, yet forget not that I am an ass. No, thou villain, thou art full of piety, as shall be proved upon thee by good witness.
> I am a wise fellow, and, which is more, an officer, and, which is more, a householder, and, which is more, as pretty a piece of flesh as any is in Messina, and one that knows the law, go to; and a rich fellow enough, go to; and a fellow that hath had losses, and one that hath two gowns and every thing handsome about him. Bring him away. O that I had been writ down an ass!

"Dost thou not suspect my place?" must have been a particularly galling question for a man in Conrad's position; his status was both above and below that of his jailer, which leaves him with no good answer to make. "Dost thou not suspect my years?" would likewise have been a tricky question to answer, because the old were above the young in the Elizabethan social hierarchy. The other items on Dogberry's resume—that he is wise, and an officer, a householder, has knowledge of the law, experience of the world, and enough worldly goods to keep him in comfort—sound, in the context of the play, as ridiculous to us as they must have sounded to Shakespeare's audiences, but Shakespeare's audiences would also have recognized them as a valid basis for Dogberry's feeling entitled to a certain amount of respect. Many people in the audience probably could not have claimed to own two gowns, or to have any knowledge of the law. But almost everyone in the audience must have felt, at one time or another, the injustice of having to grovel before people who were younger than they, less experienced, less qualified for their position, less honest, simply because of the accident of having been born on a lower rung of the social ladder. Shakespeare's audiences would have laughed at Dogberry, but they also thoroughly enjoyed the spectacle of Conrad seething and writhing in jail under Dogberry's power.

The first meeting of Angelo and Isabella in *Measure for Measure* offers us another, far less comical opportunity to examine Shakespeare's attitude towards power and its uses. In this play, the famously incorruptible judge Angelo has been elevated suddenly by the Duke of Vienna to stand in his place and rule the city. It is up to Angelo to begin enforcing Vienna's mortally severe law against fornication, even though no one has been prosecuted or condemned for such crimes in many years. When Angelo orders the arrest and execution of a young nobleman named Claudio, who has impregnated his lover Juliet, Claudio's sister Isabella come to plead his case, and there follows a nuanced conversation on how power ought to be used by those who have it, and what role mercy plays in tempering justice:

> ISABELLA
> I do think that you might pardon him,
> And neither heaven nor man grieve at the mercy.
>
> ANGELO
> I will not do't.
>
> ISABELLA
> But can you, if you would?
>
> ANGELO
> He's sentenced; 'tis too late.
>
> ISABELLA
> Too late? why, no; I, that do speak a word.

> May call it back again. Well, believe this,
> No ceremony that to great ones 'longs,
> Not the king's crown, nor the deputed sword,
> The marshal's truncheon, nor the judge's robe,
> Become them with one half so good a grace
> As mercy does.
> If he had been as you and you as he,
> You would have slipt like him; but he, like you,
> Would not have been so stern.

Isabella is in a difficult position; as a chaste maiden, on the point of entering a convent, it looks bad for her to be defending her brother's sexual misconduct. But she acknowledges this fact skillfully, then swiftly shifts the terms of the argument away from justice—which, she has no option but to agree, Claudio has fallen foul of—to mercy, a heavenly virtue which she can extol with no risk to her modesty.

Through Isabella, Shakespeare points out that, though it may not be a common person's place to make or carry out the laws, those whose place it is have the power to exercise their own judgment as to *how* the laws are carried out. In other words, Angelo, and people like him, are not excused from personal responsibility just because they wield power in the name of their lord or king. The monarch is answerable to God alone for their actions, but everyone else, including the prince's deputy, must be guided by their own conscience as well by the laws of the land. "If he had been as you and you as he"—that is, if Claudio were in charge of Vienna, and Angelo was the one who had gotten his longtime girlfriend pregnant—"you would have slipt like him; but he, like you, would not have been so stern." That is, Claudio would have shown mercy, even if Claudio had been charged with the responsibility Angelo now has for carrying out the law.

What is remarkable about this scene is that Shakespeare answers Isabella's argument for mercy with a reasonable, even penetrating response from Angelo. Angelo is no brute; he has elegant powers of reason, and, at this point in the play, it might be presumed that he is still honest (though the moment where he slips is not far off.)

> ISABELLA
> Yet show some pity.
>
> ANGELO
> I show it most of all when I show justice;
> For then I pity those I do not know,

> Which a dismiss'd offence would after gall;
> And do him right that, answering one foul wrong,
> Lives not to act another. Be satisfied;
> Your brother dies to-morrow; be content.
>
> ISABELLA
> So you must be the first that gives this sentence,
> And he, that suffer's. O, it is excellent
> To have a giant's strength; but it is tyrannous
> To use it like a giant.

There is genuine substance to Angelo's "I show [pity] most of all when I show justice"; for him, the very impersonality of his judgments is a sign of their merit. There is a reason fornication is against the law, after all; the laws encompassed more than a nobleman sleeping with his beloved before marriage, but also extended to prostitution, the spread of deadly venereal diseases, and the abundance of unwanted children who were mired in a world of poverty and violence, and who were born condemned to live blighted lives, incapable of ever escaping the stigma of bastardry.

Shakespeare was no revolutionary. He writes with sympathy about the prostitutes and bawds who are soon to be out of work when Angelo completes his project of tearing down all the public houses in Vienna, but he does not challenge the system that condemns them. He merely points out, via Isabella, that "it is excellent / to have a giant's strength; but it is tyrannous/ to use it like a giant." People in authority should be wary of how severely they insist on law and order, because there is always another giant with a bigger club, and if their lives were up for strict examination, who is to say they would not be forfeit to justice themselves? "Use every man after his desert and who shall 'scape whipping?" Hamlet demands of Polonius, when a troupe of actors comes to the court of Elsinore. There is probably no more succinct summary than this of Shakespeare's feelings about law, power, and authority, and how they ought to be exercised. Soon after his initial meeting with Isabella, Angelo, tempted for what he acknowledges is the first time in his life, fails the test, and attempts to rape Isabella by coercion; he does not know that his crime will shortly be found out by the Duke, or that the Duke will expose him for it before an appreciative crowd of commoners. If Angelo had allowed himself to be swayed by Isabella's plea for mercy, he would have escaped that mortifying fate; Shakespeare was framing a lesson there for those who had eyes to see it.

Shakespeare's earliest plays

There is no way to be completely certain as to the chronology of Shakespeare's plays—that is, to know in what order they were written. There are various theories as to which was his first play. Some scholars believe that the first dramatic work Shakespeare wrote circa 1590 was something now referred to as the "Ur-Hamlet", an early version of *Hamlet* of which there are no surviving copies, and about which nothing is known, save that it contained a character by the name of Hamlet, a ghost, and centered on a theme of revenge. (*Ur* is a Germanic prefix that indicates ancient origin.) That such a play existed we know nearly for certain, but some scholars believe it to have been the work of Thomas Kyd, rather than Shakespeare. It is possible that the "Ur-Hamlet" was an early, unsatisfying effort of Shakespeare's which he revised later, thought it also possible that he merely poached the text of another author's work for his own purposes.

Other controversial candidates for Shakespeare's earliest play include *Two Gentlemen of Verona* and *The Taming of the Shrew*. Shakespeare scholar Stanley Wells argues that *Two Gentlemen of Verona* betrays "an uncertainty of technique suggestive of inexperience"; the play also contains what is arguably a reference to another Elizabethan drama, *Midas,* by John Lyly, which was written around 1588 or 1589. There is, of course, no reason why Shakespeare could not have written *Two Gentlemen* several years after *Midas* was first performed and have simply alluded to the older work, though it certainly proves that Shakespeare was writing no earlier than 1588. Dating *The Taming of the Shrew,* on the other hand, is complicated by the fact that a play entitled *The Taming of a Shrew* was published in 1594, and scholars cannot determine whether this was an earlier version of Shakespeare's play or a different play that took its plot from the same original source. It is widely accepted, however, that Shakespeare must have written his play between August of 1592 and June of 1593; stage directions refer to an actor who died before the earlier date, and another play by Anthony Chute which directly alludes to Shakespeare's *Shrew* was performed on the latter date.

Most anthologies and reference books list Shakespeare's plays in the order set down by eminent scholar of Elizabethan drama E.K. Chambers, which lists *2 Henry VI* as Shakespeare's first play, with *3 Henry VI* and *1 Henry VI* following. Chambers' assumption is that Shakespeare would have written the first two plays between 1590 and 1591, and the third between 1591 and 1592.

The basis for his reasoning lies in the fact that Shakespeare first re-emerges in the historical record in London in 1592, via a satirical pamphlet written by Robert Greene entitled *Greene's Groats-worth of Wit*. Greene writes an allegorical tale of two brothers, one of whom, like the author, turns out badly because he falls into a career of writing plays. Greene ends the story by exhorting three young unnamed actors of his acquaintance to heed the example of the witty brother, and find some means of earning a living other than the theater. The three unnamed actors are "a famous gracer of Tragedians", "a young Juvenal", and "an upstart Crow, beautified with our feathers, that with his Tygers hart wrapt in a Players hyde" who "supposes he is as well able to bombast out a blanke verse as the best of you: and being an absolute Iohannes fac totum, is in his owne conceit the onely Shake-scene in a countrey."

"Iohannes fac totum" is Latin for "jack of all trades", which Shakespere certainly was; "Shake-scene" is convincingly similar to "Shakespeare". But most importantly, "his Tygers hart wrapt in a

Players hyde" is an unmistakable allusion to what must already have been a famous line found in Shakespeare's *3 Henry VI,* in which the evil queen, Margaret of Anjou, presents the Duke of York with a handkerchief stained with the blood of his son Rutland. York rails against her, saying:

> O tiger's heart wrapped in a woman's hide!
> How couldst thou drain the lifeblood of the child,
> To bid the father wipe his eyes withal,
> And yet be seen to bear a woman's face?
> Women are soft, mild, pitiful, and flexible;
> Thou stern, obdurate, flinty, rough, remorseless.

This is where the seven year long gap in Shakespeare's paper-trail picks back up: with Shakespeare already well-established in the world of the London theater, famous enough that Greene expected that his readers would instantly recognize an allusion to a specific line in one of his earliest plays. Assuming that Shakespeare did indeed leave Stratford shortly after the birth of his twin children in 1585, and that he came to London as part of an acting troupe, this timeline would provide him with five years to accustom himself to life in the theatrical world, establish his reputation as an actor, and then begin writing in earnest at around the turn of the decade. This would mean that he was composing the first lines of the *Henry VI* cycle just as Christopher Marlowe was achieving fame as the author of *Tamburlaine* in 1590.

That Shakespeare was paying close attention to what Marlowe was doing in the early 1590's is evident based on the striking influence of Marlowe's style on the *Henry VI* plays. It is so striking that many Marlowe scholars (to say nothing of Marlovian anti-Stratfordians) believe that Marlowe wrote parts of *Henry VI,* or that he wrote all of it and Shakespeare revised the text. Generally speaking, Shakespeare scholars do not think much of the *Henry VI* cycle of plays, apart from *Richard III,* which probably was not intended to be performed alongside the others, but which is often categorized with them because it is the logical conclusion to the story—Henry VI was deposed by the Duke of York, who became Richard III and was deposed in turn by Henry Tudor, who became Henry VII, father of Henry VIII and grandfather of Queen Elizabeth. For those familiar with Shakespeare's later works, parts of *Henry VI* do strike a somewhat jarring note. But audiences at the time were obviously entranced, and if Shakespeare was indeed imitating Marlowe intentionally (it seems impossible that he was not) then he was imitating a person who had achieved the success that he longed for. If theater-goers wanted Marlowe, he would give them something like Marlowe. Consider the opening lines of *1 Henry VI:*

> Hung be the heavens with black, yield day to night!
> Comets, importing change of times and states,
> Brandish your crystal tresses in the sky,
> And with them scourge the bad revolting stars
> That have consented unto Henry's death!
> King Henry the Fifth, too famous to live long!
> England ne'er lost a king of so much worth.

And compare them to the following passage from Tamburlaine:

> Meet heaven and earth, and here let all things end,
> For earth hath spent the pride of all her fruit,
> And heaven consum'd his choicest living fire!
> Let earth and heaven his timeless death deplore,
> For both their worths will equal him no more.

In both cases, the character speaking the lines is mourning a dead hero of legendary quality, which may account for the some of the similarity. After all, neither Marlowe nor Shakespeare were the first writers in history to conjure a vision of heavenly portents appearing to mark the death of a powerful king; this was a tradition that went back to ancient Greece and Rome. But it seems likely that Shakespeare was in attendance at one of the earliest performances of *Tamburlaine,* and that it made a powerful impression on him. This may even have been the moment in which he realized that he could achieve greater success as a writer than as an actor. We do not know a great deal about Shakespeare's acting career, but what we do know suggests that he was a character actor, rather than a leading man. Tradition has it that one of Shakespeare's best-remembered performances was that of the ghost of Hamlet's father.

We know that the Henry VI plays did wonders for Shakespeare's reputation because when Robert Greene died, not long after Greene's Groats-worth of Wit was published, his editor, Henry Chettle, thought fit to issue an apology to Shakespeare, in the preface to another publication, entitled *Kind-Heart's Dream:*

"About three months since died M. Robert Greene, leaving many papers in sundry booksellers' hands, among other his *Groatsworth of Wit,* in which a letter written to divers play-makers is offensively by one or two of them taken, and because on the dead they cannot be avenged, they willfully forge in their conceits a living author.... With neither of them that take offence was I acquainted, and with one of them I care not if I never be. The other, whom at that time I did not so much spare as since I wish I had, for that, as I have moderated the heat of living writers and might have used my own discretion (especially in such a case, the author being dead), that I did not I am as sorry as if the original fault had been my fault, because myself have seen his demeanor no less civil than he excellent in the quality he professes. Besides, the diver of worship have reported his uprightness of dealing, which argues his honesty, and his facetious grace in writing that approves his art."

The fact that Chettle saw fit to single Shakespeare out for an apology, when he did not bother to do so for the other two nascent playwrights lampooned by Greene, suggests that Shakespeare had already established himself as a force to be reckoned—and that he was probably already gathering to himself powerful friends and connections, even patrons.

Chapter Four: Shakespeare's People

Christopher Marlowe

Greenblatt suggests that Shakespeare might have figured out early in his career that he was not a sufficiently gifted actor to compete in the same league as the brilliant leading man who originated the role of Tamburlaine, which is why he turned to writing at around the same time this play was first being performed. This is a convincing theory, if only because the first contemporary references to Shakespeare, like Robert Greene's, alluded to his reputation as a writer. If Shakespeare had confined himself to acting, it is possible that we would never have heard of him at all. Marlowe was the writer who first employed blank verse—unrhymed iambic pentameter—as the dramatic medium for his plays, and Shakespeare must have understood that *Tamburlaine's* power stemmed in part from the relentless, beating rhythm of its structure, because he ran with the suggestion when he began writing his own plays.

Marlowe and Shakespeare had enough in common that Shakespeare probably could not have helped comparing himself to the more successful playwright. Marlowe was born the same year as Shakespeare, in 1564 in the town of Canterbury, which was fairly similar to Stratford. John Marlowe, Christopher's father, was a shoemaker, an almost poetic parallel to John Shakespeare's trade of glovemaker. Marlowe had attended what was once a cathedral school, rebranded as a Protestant institution under Edward VI, like Shakespeare's grammar school, which was founded by Stratford's Catholic guild and rebranded after the dissolution of the monasteries. At this point, however, their careers diverged for a time; Marlowe went to Cambridge, where he was an undergraduate on scholarship at Corpus Christi and received his degree in 1584, around the time Shakespeare was preparing for the birth of his two younger children. One wonders whether Shakespeare winced when he learned that his role-model and possible rival had this advantage over him in education. Had Shakespeare completed his education at grammar school, it is possible that he too might have gone on to Oxford or Cambridge, assuming his father's financial situation had permitted it. We have no indication that Shakespeare regretted this lost opportunity, but it may well have crossed his mind that if he had received a higher education like Marlowe's, he would have been just as successful.

Marlowe was a person it would have been impossible for Shakespeare not to envy in the early 1590's. He had written his first play, *Dido, Queen of Carthage,* in about 1587, though it was not performed in London; *Tamburlaine* was his first play performed in the theaters, and it was a runaway success. This was followed by *The Jew of Malta,* and *Edward II, The Massacre at Paris,* about the St. Bartholomew's Day slaughter of French Huguenots, a relatively recent event which had incensed Protestants in England, and *Doctor Faustus,* in which a scholar in search of wisdom sells his soul to the devil. All of these plays were written and performed between 1588 and 1593. It is an extremely impressive body of work for so young a man, and Shakespeare must have felt that he had his work cut out for him if he was ever to rival it.

Though Marlowe, like Shakespeare, took historical sources for the plots of his plays, Shakespeare was not particularly interested in serious scholarship. He tended to skim the works of historical writers, like Holinshed, for the characters and events that appeared in his drama, whereas Marlowe read extensively, plumbing obscure scholars and sources for his dramatic material, including the works of Asian writers whose scholarship had not been translated into English. Marlowe's university education would have habituated him to libraries and research, and he would have had the leisure as an undergraduate to acquaint himself with a wide body of literature—a marked contrast to Shakespeare, for whom books would have been an expensive indulgence.

Scholars have speculated for centuries as to what Marlowe got up to when he wasn't writing plays. An entire cottage industry of myth-making, known as "the Marlowe legend", had sprung up around his imagined exploits. He is rumored to have been an atheist (a genuinely shocking accusation in the Elizabethan era), gay or bisexual, and, most interestingly of all, a spy for the English government. Much of this speculation is based on the content of his plays and the mysterious manner of his death. *Tamburlaine* rejected the entire Elizabethan system of morality and piety, by asserting that the pursuit of power was the noblest ambition a man could pursue; it presumably shocked some of those who saw it performed, and led him to wonder what sort of man might have written it. Marlowe undoubtedly had secrets. When he was scheduled to receive a master's degree from Oxford (bachelor's degrees at this automatically converted into master's after a few years) the university authorities were hesitant to grant it, because there were rumors that he had traveled to France with the intention of becoming a Catholic priest. But the misunderstanding was cleared up due to the direct intervention of the Privy Council, who commended him for unnamed services to the Queen.

The nature of those services have engendered enormous speculation. Francis Walsingham, Queen Elizabeth's personal secretary, employed a vast network of spies who provided him with the intelligence he needed to remain one step ahead of Catholic conspiracies against the throne. Because Walsingham paid his informants out of his own pocket, there were no official records of their movements or missions in most cases. Marlowe, therefore, may well have been one of these spies. The Cambridge authorities were assured that Marlowe had traveled to France on "matters touching the benefit of his country", so he was certainly employed by the government in some secret capacity.

Then, in May of 1593, Marlowe was arrested over the matter of the "Dutch church libel". Elizabethan politics in the 1590's were dominated by the plight of Protestants in the Netherlands who were seeking independence, under the banner of William of Orange, from the

Catholic King Philip of Spain. Philip was known to be the silent backer of multiple plots to invade England, rally Elizabeth's Catholic subjects to overthrow her, and place Mary Stuart, Queen of Scots, on the throne in her place. Elizabeth knew that the Spanish troupes which had been dispatched to the Netherlands to quell the Protestant uprising were conveniently placed to launch an invasion of England, and indeed, during the invasion of the Spanish Armada, they were poised to do so. All loyal Englishmen were therefore expected to support the plight of Dutch Protestants, so it looked very bad for Marlowe when the following poem was plastered on doors and walls about London, addressed to refugee Dutchmen living in the city:

> Ye strangers yt doe inhabite in this lande
> Note this same writing doe it vnderstand
> Conceit it well for savegard of your lyves
> Your goods, your children, & your dearest wives
> Your Machiavellian Marchant spoyles the state,
> Your vsery doth leave vs all for deade
> Your Artifex, & craftsman works our fate,
> And like the Jewes, you eate us vp as bread
> The Marchant doth ingross all kinde of wares

    Forestall's the markets, whereso 'ere he goe's
    Sends forth his wares, by Pedlers to the faires,
    Retayle's at home, & with his horrible showes:
    Vndoeth thowsands
    In Baskets your wares trott up & downe
    Carried the streets by the country nation,
    You are intelligencers to the state & crowne
    And in your hartes doe wish an alteracion,
    You transport goods, & bring vs gawds good store
    Our Leade, our Vittaile, our Ordenance & what nott
    That Egipts plagues, vext not the Egyptians more
    Then you doe vs; then death shall be your lotte
    Noe prize comes in but you make claime therto
    And every merchant hath three trades at least,
    And Cutthrote like in selling you vndoe us all, & with our store continually you feast: We cannot suffer long.
    Our pore artificers doe starve & dye
    For yt they cannot now be sett on worke
    And for your worke more curious to the ey[.]
    In Chambers, twenty in one house will lurke,

        Raysing of rents, was never knowne before
        Living farre better then at native home
        And our pore soules, are cleane thrust out of dore
        And to the warres are sent abroade to rome,
        To fight it out for Fraunce & Belgia,
        And dy like dogges as sacrifice for you
        Expect you therefore such a fatall day
        Shortly on you, & yours for to ensewe: as never was seene.
        Since words nor threates nor any other thinge
        canne make you to avoyd this certaine ill
        Weele cutte your throtes, in your temples praying
        Not paris massacre so much blood did spill
        As we will doe iust vengeance on you all
        In counterfeitinge religion for your flight
        When 't'is well knowne, you are loth, for to be thrall
        your coyne, & you as countryes cause to flight
        With Spanish gold, you all are infected
        And with yt gould our Nobles wink at feats
        Nobles said I? nay men to be reiected,
        Upstarts yt enioy the noblest seates
        That wound their Countries brest, for lucres sake
        And wrong our gracious Queene & Subiects good

> By letting strangers make our harts to ake
> For which our swords are whet, to shedd their blood
> And for a truth let it be understoode
> Fly, Flye, & never returne.

Not only are there are number of references to Marlowe's plays interspersed throughout the poem—"your Machiavellian marchant" probably alludes to *The Jew of Malta*—but the text is written in Marlowe's signature blank verse, and the poet actually signed himself "Tamberlaine". The Privy Council ordered an immediate investigation, and in the process, arrested the playwright Thomas Kyd, who had once worked jointly with Marlowe on a play (possibly the so-called *Ur-Hamlet,* or a lost play which had been variously attributed to Kyd, Marlowe, and Shakespeare, called *Edward III*.) When Kyd's rooms were searched, a page from a Catholic pamphlet was discovered, and Kyd pointed the finger at Marlowe, probably under torture. Marlowe was living with a relative of Francis Walsingham's when the Privy Council ordered his arrest. On the 20th of May, 1593, Marlowe surrendered himself to the Council, only to discover that none of the councilors were available to question him; he was ordered to "give his daily attendance on their Lordships, until he shall be licensed to the contrary", that is, to keep showing up until someone was around to talk to him.

Ten days later, on May 30, 1593, Christopher Marlowe was dead. According to the *Palladis Tamia* by Francis Meres, published in 1598, he met his end in a tavern brawl:

"As Iodelle, a French tragical poet, beeing an epicure and an atheist, made a pitifull end: so our tragicall poet Marlow for his Epicurisme and Atheisme had a tragical death. You may read of this Marlow more at large in the *Theatre of God's judgments,* in the 25th chapter entreating of Epicures and Atheists. As the poet Lycophron was shot to death by a certain rival of his: so Christopher Marlow was stabd to death by a bawdy Servingman, a rival of his in his lewde love."

Hundreds of years later, the official coroner's report from the inquest into Marlowe's death was discovered, which gave a different version of events. According to the report, Marlowe had spent the day of his death in the company of three other men, all of whom worked for the Walsingham family. Two of Marlowe's companions, Nicholas Skeres and Robert Poley, had helped to foil the Babington conspiracy to assassinate the Queen. The third was a man named Ingram Frizer, with whom Marlowe began to quarrel over an unpaid bill. According to witnesses, Marlowe started the fight, lunging at Frizer with a dagger and cutting his forehead. Frizer fought back and stabbed Marlowe fatally above the right eye. The inquest determined that Frizer was acting in self-defense and did not charge him for murder. The timing of the fight, however, following so closely after Marlowe's arrest, has inspired many to wonder if the witnesses were paid, or ordered by members of the Privy Council, to testify that Marlowe died in a fight over a bill in order to cover up an assassination.

Christopher Marlowe died at the start of an extremely promising career, but to Shakespeare he must have already looked like a success. In order to compete with the Admiral's Men, who first performed *Tamburlaine* to such enormous acclaim, Shakespeare was likely inspired to write an historical epic for his own company, the Queen's Men, to stage in response. But instead of mimicking Marlowe and turning to the legendary kings of the far east for his dramatic material, he cleverly chose to write about the Wars of the Roses—a bloody period of political chaos and civil war from which, it was popularly understood, the Tudor dynasty had delivered England into its present peace and prosperity. In short, the *Henry VI* plays were flattering to the Queen, and flattering the Queen always a safe move in the Elizabethan era. Furthermore, by writing about English history, he was presenting his audiences with a story that was familiar to them. Shakespeare was not an especially original writer, but he excelled at breathing new life into old stories.

It is not surprising that the *Henry VI* plays achieved instant popularity, because Shakespeare was not just giving his audiences a fresh look at history; he was speaking to their present anxieties. Civil war was anything but a distant and long-vanquished threat to the Elizabethan mind. Henry VIII had divorced the nation from Rome and his son Edward VI had made them Protestant; at the end of his short reign, Mary I made England Catholic again, forcing the younger generation, raised in the new religion, to convert or be condemned for heresy. Then Elizabeth had come to make them Protestant again, and almost her entire reign was beset with the fear that her Catholic subjects would rise up against her and put the Queen of Scots in her place. These divisions ran deep into the heart of English society; every Protestant, it was said, had a Papist somewhere in their family, and conflicting loyalties to blood and crown ensured that the grisly specter of a new civil war haunted the mind of every thinking, feeling person. In *Tamburlaine,* Marlowe conjured a vision of a conqueror and a titan bending the world to his will; but in *Henry VI,* Shakespeare evoked the despair of a world in which order has given way to chaos. The plays are full of characters who rival Tamburlaine in their cruelty and their desire for power, but if Tamburlaine is a modern comic supervillain, then Shakespeare warring dukes, earls, and lords are nothing less than petty criminals. In Tamburlaine, to strive for and gain supreme power is glorious; in Henry VI, the appetite for power is a base urge that leads only to the destruction of the realm and the soul.

The university wits

The somewhat conservative theme of the *Henry VI* plays is relevant to Shakespeare's social life as a young poet. By age and occupation, he was the peer of a circle of poets and dramatists remembered now as "the university wits": Marlowe, Robert Greene, Thomas Lodge, John Lyly, Thomas Nash, Thomas Watson, and George Peele. They came from various social backgrounds, but all of them had attended

Oxford or Cambridge, and in a society that was just beginning to produce more educated men than it had occupations for, they had all turned their backs on respectability by opting to write for the theater, rather than pursue careers in the church or in law. They were all accomplished men of letters, writing pamphlets, translating Greek and Latin in their spare time to excite the admiration of their friends. Marlowe's extensive research into the historical Tamburlaine stands as an example of the high degree to which all of them prized literature and rarefied knowledge. And like all well-educated young men with time on their hands in any era of history, they had a bohemian contempt for all that was staid and orderly—urban life, with its aura of danger, intrigue, and violence suited them down to the ground.

These men were Shakespeare's rivals and competitors, and he was probably on friendly terms with most of them. It is inevitable that they would have known who he was after the fame of *Henry VI,* and they might even have socialized. But Shakespeare was not really a part of their circle, and it is easy to envision why. Shakespeare clearly had a voracious appetite for information and books, but he did not have the same access to libraries and the company of learned scholars that his university-educated colleagues had. He must have struck them as unpolished, even unsophisticated, unable to participate in long conversations about Latin poetic forms. And Shakespeare wasn't especially bohemian in his sentiments. *Tamburlaine,* with its vision of a new world order, was revolutionary in the strictest sense of the word; *Henry VI* was conservative, in the broadest sense, depicting a world in which the collapse of the customary social order led to nothing less than hell on earth and the slaughter of innocents.

Furthermore, unlike Marlowe and the rest, Shakespeare was anything but a carefree bachelor or the black sheep of his family. He maintained strong ties to his parents, wife, and children back in Stratford, and ordered all his financial affairs with them in mind. And some scholars are inclined to think that Shakespeare had a certain distaste for what we might now call "the party scene". Marlowe, Green, Lyly, Lodge, and the rest were habitués of taverns and whorehouses, again like most bohemian young with nothing but themselves and their careers to care for. Shakespeare, however, writes with great feeling about drunkenness and drunkards in his plays; in the *Henry IV* plays, Falstaff, though brilliant and great-hearted, is a portrait of a man who has wasted his tremendous powers by life-long habits of overindulgence. And there is a remarkable speech in Scene IV of *Hamlet,* where Shakespeare seems to give way to a long-repressed urge to condemn revelry wholesale:

> HORATIO
> (A flourish of trumpets, and ordnance shot off, within)
> What does this mean, my lord?
>
> HAMLET
> The king doth wake to-night and takes his rouse,
> Keeps wassail, and the swaggering up-spring reels;
> And, as he drains his draughts of Rhenish down,
> The kettle-drum and trumpet thus bray out
> The triumph of his pledge.
>
> HORATIO
> Is it a custom?
>
> HAMLET
> Ay, marry, is't:
> But to my mind, though I am native here
> And to the manner born, it is a custom
> More honour'd in the breach than the observance.
> This heavy-headed revel east and west
> Makes us traduced and tax'd of other nations:

> They clepe us drunkards, and with swinish phrase
> Soil our addition; and indeed it takes
> From our achievements, though perform'd at height,
> The pith and marrow of our attribute.
> So, oft it chances in particular men,
> That for some vicious mole of nature in them,
> As, in their birth--wherein they are not guilty,
> Since nature cannot choose his origin--
> By the o'ergrowth of some complexion,
> Oft breaking down the pales and forts of reason,
> Or by some habit that too much o'er-leavens
> The form of plausive manners, that these men,
> Carrying, I say, the stamp of one defect,
> Being nature's livery, or fortune's star,--
> Their virtues else--be they as pure as grace,
> As infinite as man may undergo--
> Shall in the general censure take corruption
> From that particular fault: the dram of eale
> Doth all the noble substance of a doubt
> To his own scandal.

This is a remarkably strange speech, appearing as it does at a moment when Hamlet's mind is otherwise fixed on the promise of seeing his father's ghost appear on the platform outside the castle. It is memorable, both for the strength of its language and because it feels out of place, a distraction from the otherwise eerie mood of the scene. The very next line heralds the arrival of the ghost, and one gets the sense that Hamlet's father has saved Hamlet's companions from having to think up something to say in reply to a deeply awkward moment. Some scholars have theorized that Shakespeare's extended meditation on the overuse of alcohol is an indication that John Shakespeare's abrupt reversal of fortune in Shakespeare's boyhood was at least partially attributable to the onset of alcoholism. If John Shakespeare was afflicted with that disease, it would explain a great many things—such as why, after a long and respectable term of service as an alderman, he simply stopped attending meetings, and why his fellow aldermen kept him on the rolls for a few months despite the fact that nonattendance was normally grounds for much swifter termination. It is as if they held out hope that he would return to his senses. And the drunkards who appear in Shakespeare's plays are often paternal figures, like Falstaff and Claudius.

Perhaps the strongest argument for Shakespeare's having been moderate and circumscribed in his habits, to the apparent distaste of the university wits, is the historical evidence we possess which points to his having had an extraordinary work ethic with all the self-discipline necessary to, in the words of one scholar:

"...manage the affairs of his playing company, to write steadily (not to mention brilliantly) for more than two decades, to accumulate and keep a great deal of money, to stay out of prison and to avoid ruinous lawsuits, to invest in agricultural land and in London property, to purchase one of the finest houses in the town where he was born, and to retire to that town in his late forties."

He goes on to point out that "this pattern of behavior did not suddenly and belatedly emerge; it established itself early, probably quite soon after the turbulent, confused, painful years that led up to his escape from Stratford and his arrival in London."

Shakespeare's plays outshine the work produced by his peers, and considering how talented and highly educated they were, it must have galled them when they began to realize that a country bumpkin with only a smattering of Latin and the merest passing acquaintance with Greek, was outstripping them artistically. Rarefied though their tastes may have been, they were writing casually, producing poetry and drama in between bouts of drinking and late-night debates on religion and politics. Shakespeare, by comparison, wrote at a steady place of two extraordinary plays per year for his entire career. And he seems to have had a reputation for being trustworthy about money, because by 1594 he was already acting as a sort of treasury for his company. No one would have trusted Robert Greene to look after money that belonged to the whole group.

When Robert Greene died in 1592, he was penniless, and only escaped dying in the street because a poor shoemaker and his wife took him in and looked after him for his last few days. Thomas Watson died the same year, probably of plague, and Marlowe was killed a few months after that. George Peele lived long enough to write poems in tribute to Watson and Marlowe's deaths, but then he died in 1596. Out of all the university wits, only Thomas Lodge escaped an early and ignominious death, and he accomplished this by the expedient of turning his back on the bohemian lifestyle he and his circle of friends had cherished and going into practice as a doctor. These deaths left Shakespeare without any serious rivals. As "poets", they had looked down on actors, which is why Robert Greene accused Shakespeare of being "wrapped in a Player's hyde"—it was seen as effrontery in him to be writing plays when he ought to content himself with acting in them. But it was the actor turned author who would outlive them, and so overshadow their reputations as to relegate them to obscurity. Greenblatt imagines that Shakespeare had the university wits in mind when he wrote, in *I Henry IV*, a scene in which the young Prince Hal tells himself that he will be content to keep company with Falstaff and his company of tavern frequenters for a time,

> "...and will a while uphold
> The unyoked humour of your idleness.
> Yet herein will I imitate the sun,
> Who doth permit the base contagious clouds
> To smother up his beauty from the world,
> That when he please again to be himself,
> Being wanted he may be more wondered at
> By breaking through the foul and ugly mists
> Of vapours that did seem to strange him."

Hal keeps this quiet promise to himself when he spurns Falstaff in the play's sequel, *2 Henry IV*, and casts off his debauched companions to take his place at his father's side, the "sun" (or "son) revealed at last. Perhaps Shakespeare had similar feelings about Marlowe, Greene, and the rest, a sense that, though it was they who looked down on him, it was he who did not truly belong in their company, because he was set apart for some higher and more solitary purpose.

Henry Wriothesley, 3rd earl of Southampton

The fact that Richard Chettle offered Shakespeare an apology for his role in printing Robert Greene's insulting epigram in Groats-worth of Wit indicates that Shakespeare had distinguished himself from his theatrical colleagues by landing himself in the good graces of someone who was important, someone who possessed the wealth and social standing necessary to engender respect, and not a little fear, into the hearts of those who were inclined to look down on his favorite poet. But who was the patron?

No personal correspondence of Shakespeare's survives, no letters to the family he left behind in

Stratford or the friends and business associates he knew in London. The closest approximation we have to an intimate letter of Shakespeare's are the dedications that preface his two romantic poems, *Venus and Adonis* and *The Rape of Lucrece,* and these were both addressed to a young nobleman, Henry Wriothesley, the third early of Southampton. We do not know when or how Shakespeare and Southampton first met; all that we know of their relationship is what can be divined from these dedications.

The first dedication, from *Venus and Adonis,* seems to have been written before the poet and the young lord met, or at least before Shakespeare felt certain that he had any claim on Southampton's loyalty. The dedication is formal in tone, and was clearly written in an attempt to win the younger man's favor (and thus his financial assistance.)

"I know not how I shall offend in dedicating my unpolished lines to your lordship, nor how the world will censure me for choosing so strong a prop to support so weak a burden: Only, if your honour seem but pleased, I account myself highly praised, and vow to take advantage of all idle hours, till I have honoured you with some graver labour. But if the first heir of my invention prove deformed, I shall be sorry it had so noble a god-father, and never after ear so barren a land, for fear it yield me still so bad a harvest. I leave it to your honourable survey, and your honour to your heart's content: which I wish may always answer your wish, and the world's hopeful expectation."

Venus and Adonis was written in 1592; about a year later, Shakespeare fulfilled his promise to honor Southampton with "some graver labour", publishing *The Rape of Lucrece* with the following dedication:

"The love I dedicate to your lordship is without end; whereof this pamphlet, without beginning, is but a superfluous moiety. The warrant I have of your honourable disposition, not the worth of my untutored lines, makes it assured of acceptance. What I have done is yours; what I have to do is yours; being part in all I have, devoted yours. Were my worth greater, my duty would show greater; meantime, as it is, it is bound to your lordship, to whom I wish long life, still lengthened with all happiness."

The shift in tone is remarkable. The first dedication is written by an uncertain poet to a powerful stranger who, as far as Shakespeare knows, is as likely to be offended by the offer of a poem as to be flattered. The second is written by a man who, judging strictly by the text, seems to be in love with his patron, and to expect no return for his love. It is largely for this reason that scholars have traditionally associated Southampton with the beautiful young man to whom a great many of Shakespeare's sonnets are addressed. But based on what we know of Southampton's life, Shakespeare may have been moved to write poetry about him for another reason.

In his biography of Shakespeare, Nicholas Rowe writes that,

"There is one instance so singular in the magnificence of this patron of Shakespeare that, if I had not been assured that the story was handed down by Sir William D'Avenant, who was probably very well acquainted with his affairs, I should not have ventured to have inserted; that my Lord Southampton at one time gave him a thousand pounds to enable him to go through with a purchase which he heard he had a mind to."

A thousand pounds, in Shakespeare's time, is equivalent to about five thousand pounds today, or around eight thousand dollars. Southampton was extremely wealthy and had a reputation for being somewhat careless, if not reckless, with his money. And he was in a tricky legal position in the early 1590's. His parents had undergone a bitter divorce when he was a small boy and his mother, who was charged with adultery, was forbidden to see him or have anything to do with his upbringing. The young Henry was placed in the household of William Cecil, Lord Burghley, who was Elizabeth I's most trusted advisor. Because Burghley was his guardian, Southampton was legally required either to marry the person Burghley chose for him, or pay a stupendous fine of five thousand pounds. When Burghley arranged a marriage between Southampton and a girl who just happened to be Burghley's own granddaughter, Southampton, who was only sixteen years old at the time, flatly refused to go through with the union.

Southampton claimed that he had no objections to the prospective bride herself, but that he could not stomach the idea of marrying anyone. His family, terrified by the prospect of losing a huge sum of money to legal fines, tried everything in their power to persuade him, but Southampton was too wealthy and too careless about money for any financially-based arguments to persuade him. Some scholars have speculated that when all other attempts at persuasion failed, they made a last-ditch effort and turned to an unconventional source: poetry. Southampton was known to be a great admirer of plays and the theater, and thus it is entirely possible that he had attended performances of *Henry VI or Titus Andronicus* and come to admire Shakespeare as an actor or writer before Shakespeare wrote *Venus and Adonis* and dedicated it to him. It is also possible, some have theorized, that Southampton's family, or perhaps even someone in Burghley's household, approached Shakespeare with the offer of an unusual commission: to write a series of poems specifically calculated to appeal to a young man's sense of romance and soften him towards the idea of marriage.

If this was the case, and Shakespeare was motivated, for some reason, to win Southampton to the cause of marriage at the behest of his guardians, it would explain the unusual argument that appears in some of the sonnets, of which Sonnet 10 is the clearest example:

> For shame deny that thou bear'st love to any,
> Who for thy self art so unprovident.
> Grant, if thou wilt, thou art beloved of many,
> But that thou none lov'st is most evident:

> For thou art so possessed with murderous hate,
> That 'gainst thy self thou stick'st not to conspire,
> Seeking that beauteous roof to ruinate
> Which to repair should be thy chief desire.
> O! change thy thought, that I may change my mind:
> Shall hate be fairer lodged than gentle love?
> Be, as thy presence is, gracious and kind,
> Or to thyself at least kind-hearted prove:
> Make thee another self for love of me,
> That beauty still may live in thine or thee.

Traditionally, the writer of sonnets wrote to win the love of a woman who had behaved coldly towards him, or examine his own enraptured or despairing emotional state. Never, before Shakespeare, had anyone written a sonnet which, like this one, exhorts a beautiful young man to marry a woman so that he can have a child that looks just like him, thus preserving his beauty for posterity. But even if the Southampton family employed Shakespeare to fit the mind of their wayward and theater-mad heir for marriage via poetry, it seems as though the relationship progressed to a condition of some intimacy, at least on Shakespeare's side. It is one thing to press a young man to "make thee another self", but it is quite another to ask him to do so "for love of me". Shakespeare, clearly, is emotionally invested in the object of his sonnets, but he seems to feel that he has grounds for believing that the beloved object is at least somewhat emotionally invested in him.

Whether or not Southampton had the same feelings for Shakespeare that Shakespeare had for him—and whatever the nature of those feelings were—poems like *Venus and Adonis* and *The Rape of Lucrece* were important to Shakespeare's career. Plague killed off hundreds or thousands of Londoners every summer, and because medicine was less a science in the Elizabethan era than a collection of superstitious rituals, no one understood how it was transmitted. All they knew was that infected persons could pass it along to uninfected persons, which is why the unlucky sufferers were usually boarded up alive in their homes. There was also an understanding that crowds facilitated the spread of the disease, so any establishment that routinely drew a crowd, like the theaters, was subject to peremptory closings. A troupe of players had only two options when the theaters were non-operational: either they could travel the countryside and try their luck staging performances from town to town, or they could, if they were very fortunate, ask their wealthy patrons for enough money to tide them over. Because *Venus and Adonis* and *The Rape of Lucrece* were written during a period in which the theaters were closed in 1593, we can surmise that his application for patronage was successful, and that Southampton probably kept him afloat until the theaters re-opened. This generosity, combined with Southampton's famously delicate, feminine good looks, may well have stirred the heart of the poet to some tender feelings towards him.

Chapter Five: Shakespeare at Home

Death of Hamnet Shakespeare

Hamnet Shakespeare, the poet's only son, died in 1596, at the age of eleven. The cause of his death was not officially recorded, but it was almost certainly due to bubonic plague, which swept away so many lives in the Elizabethan era. We do not know if Shakespeare was able to see the boy before his death, or how often they had seen each other since Shakespeare left Stratford shortly after his birth. In the absence of distinct historical evidence to the contrary, it seems likely that he was at least present for Hamnet's burial in August of 1596.

Scholars have speculated broadly about the effect of his son's death, and the grief that must have followed, on Shakespeare's plays. The obvious connection that tends to be drawn is with *Hamlet,* Shakespeare's longest, strangest play, which was written in 1600, four years afterwards. Hamnet and his twin sister Judith were probably named for a married couple who were neighbors of the Shakespeare family, Hamnet and Judith Sadler; Hamnet Sadler was one of the witnesses to Shakespeare's will. But Sadler's name is sometimes recorded in parish documents, with the customary 16th century lack of regard for regular spelling, as *Hamlette*. This makes the connection between the lost son and the Danish prince seem fairly obvious. During the four years before *Hamlet* was first performed, Shakespeare wrote a series of light-hearted comedies, including *The Merry Wives of Windsor* and *Much Ado About Nothing,* which would seem to suggest that the subject of Hamnet's death was still too fresh in Shakespeare's feelings to dwell upon at great length.

On the other hand, *King John,* which probably deserves the title of Shakespeare's strangest history play, was written in the very year of Hamnet's death, and the action of that play centers around the death of a child—Arthur, nephew of King John and potential claimant to his throne. The king is urged by his nobles to have the boy killed, and after an agonizing inward struggle, King John orders his servant Hubert to do the deed; Hubert, however, cannot bring himself to commit the murder. The king is immensely relieved when Hubert confesses this to him, but shortly afterwards he receives words that Arthur has been found dead—fearing torture, the boy has thrown himself to his death from the high battlements of the castle. No one believes the king when he claims that he had no hand in it, and he loses his crown as a consequence. The scene in which Arthur pleads with Hubert for his life is easily one of the most moving scenes Shakespeare ever wrote. And when Arthur's mother learns of his death, her grief is so extreme that it frightens all who witness it; she explains that,

> "Grief fills the room up of my absent child
> Lies in his bed, walks up and down with me,
> Puts on his pretty looks, repeats his words,
> Remembers me of all his gracious parts,
> Stuffs out his vacant garments with his form."

If *Hamlet* is the work of a brilliant artist attempting to work out the deeply ambiguous feelings which a rational person must entertain over the loss of a child in an age when one in three children were dead before the age of ten, then *King John* may be the first wild lamentations of a father seeking to vent his grief. *Hamlet,* after all, is anything but straightforward on the subject of father-son relationships; *King John,* on the other hand, is full of the uncomplicated horror that the death of a child engenders in adults who care for him.

Shakespeare the businessman

Today, Shakespeare's name is virtually synonymous with the name of the Globe, the theater where so many of his plays were performed by the Lord Chamberlain's Men, but casual students of literature are rarely aware just how direct a role Shakespeare played in its construction. Until 1598, Shakespeare's troupe had performed their plays in a theater (named "The Theatre") which had been built in 1576 by the father of the Lord Chamberlain's principle leading man, Richard Burbage, on land owned by one Giles Allen. When Burbage died around the time that the lease on the land expired, his sons attempted to negotiate a renewal, but were unable to come to terms with Allen.

So it was that on December 28, 1598, the players of the Lord Chamberlain's Men—Shakespeare possibly among them—stole, in the dead of night, to the site of the Theatre, and dismantled the building timber by timber. It was a remarkable feat, even considering that the actors were all equipped with the axes, swords, and other weaponry they used in their productions, and that the whole operation was overseen by the company's carpenter, Peter Street. The wood from the Theatre was stored at Street's home until the spring of 1599, when it was used in the construction a new playhouse—the first in London designed and built by the players themselves. Giles Allen, understandably, was infuriated, but as it turned out, he could do nothing about it—the terms of the original lease explicitly stated that any structure which Burbage built on Allen's land belonged to him, and not Allen.

This was the beginning of Shakespeare's second career as a businessman and investor in property. He became the owner of one-tenth of the Globe's interests, and it was on the basis of this investment that he was to become a wealthy man. He had already earned enough money to have purchased New Place in Stratford by 1597, the largest house in town, boasting twenty rooms. He may also have been something of a moneylender on the side; there are records of businessmen in Stratford approaching him for loans. He would also eventually acquire a tavern called the Maidenhead, also in Stratford. It was probably on the strength of this financial success that Shakespeare renewed his father's application for a coat of arms in 1596. The motto

Shakespeare claimed was "non sanz droit", or "not without right", as though he felt a little defensive about the prospect of claiming a gentleman's status.

A few years later, after his father's death, Shakespeare applied to have the Shakespeare arms quartered, or displayed with, the Arden coat of arms, asserting his connection to the ancient family from which his mother was descended. John Shakespeare had about six years to enjoy this elevation of his status before he died in 1602. After his death, one of the heralds of the College of Arms made a formal complaint that within the past few years, arms had been issued to twenty-three persons who were unworthy of the honor. By this time, Shakespeare was the head of his family, and his name—listed as "Shakespeare ye player"—appeared near the top of the list of supposedly unworthy persons. The challenge had to be answered, but John Shakespeare's claim to gentility was reaffirmed by the College's most senior herald, who pointed to the fact that the elder Shakespeare had once been the Bailiff of Stratford, and repeating John Shakespeare's claim that his grandfather had been honored by Henry VII for fighting in the Battle of Bosworth Field.

The Retirement and Death of William Shakespeare

In 1610, after writing over thirty plays, 154 sonnets, two epic poems, and probably other plays and poems that have not survived, William Shakespeare retired to Stratford to live with his family and enjoy the fruits of two decades of labor in the world of the London theater. Those fruits were considerable, and he gained them by paying close attention to his business interests. In the fame "gravedigger scene" in *Hamlet,* Shakespeare reveals an intimate knowledge of technical terms associated with property law, when Hamlet examines a skull and wonders if,

"This fellow might be in 's time a great buyer of land, with his statutes, his recognizances, his fines, his double-vouchers, his recoveries Is this the fine of his fines and the recovery of his recoveries, to have his fine pate full of fine dirt? Will his vouchers vouch him no more of his purchases, and double ones too, than the length and breadth of a pair of indentures? The very conveyances of his lands will hardly lie in this box; and must th'inheritor himself have no more, ha?"

Shakespeare, at various points throughout his body of plays, manages to sound like a doctor, a lawyer, a soldier, etc., and there is no indication that he ever undertook any of those professions. But he was a great investor in real estate, and he no doubt came by his knowledge of these legal terms first-hand.

By 1603, Shakespeare's company, the Lord Chamberlain's Men, were the pre-eminent theatrical troupe in London. After the death of Elizabeth I, they received the royal warrant of the new king, James I, whereupon they changed their name to the King's Men. James I ordered frequent performances of plays at the royal court, for which the company was paid excellent rates. But there was still an entire season's worth of performances to give at the Globe, which meant that Shakespeare, as the company's manager, principal author, and a player, was probably run off his heels. He may have taken a step back from acting to concentrate on writing and managing the company, but it is more likely that he was still required to perform, since the company was not large enough to do without any of its principal actors. We can guess that he probably began meditating on the possibility of retirement around 1604, when he wrote the extraordinary tragedy of *King Lear,* which dwells extensively on the loss of identity that follows a king choosing to give up his kingdom to his three daughters and their husbands.

Shakespeare's last several plays were probably written in collaboration with another member of his company, John Fletcher. The last play which he wrote entirely on his own was *The Tempest,* which tells the story of Prospero, once the Duke of Milan and now a supremely powerful magician, who has been shipwrecked on an island with only his daughter Miranda for company. Prospero uses his magic to cause a shipwreck that brings his brother Antonio, who usurped his throne, to the island; but when Miranda falls in love with Antonio's son, Ferdinand, Prospero "drowns his books", i.e. surrenders all his magical powers, and the play closes on a famous epilogue in which the sorcerer—who well might stand in for the playwright—asking the audience to give him the applause, the prayer, the good spirits and good wishes and forgiveness he needs to move on with his life:

> Now my charms are all o'erthrown,
> And what strength I have's mine own,
> Which is most faint: now, 'tis true,
> I must be here confined by you,
> Or sent to Naples. Let me not,
> Since I have my dukedom got

And pardon'd the deceiver, dwell
In this bare island by your spell;
But release me from my bands
With the help of your good hands:
Gentle breath of yours my sails
Must fill, or else my project fails,
Which was to please. Now I want
Spirits to enforce, art to enchant,
And my ending is despair,
Unless I be relieved by prayer,
Which pierces so that it assaults
Mercy itself and frees all faults.
As you from crimes would pardon'd be,
Let your indulgence set me free.

The *Tempest* was written in 1610. We don't know precisely when Shakespeare returned to Stratford to live full time, but it was probably shortly after the 1610 season ended. He did not give up playwriting entirely—he would collaborate with Fletcher on Henry VIII and *Two Noble Kinsmen* and a lost play called *Cardenio*—but for the first time since he was 22, his day to day life was lived, not amidst the bustle of Europe's second-largest metropolis, but amidst the pastoral scenes of his childhood. He was now 46 years old. Though it does not entirely fit our expectation of a brilliant artist's priorities, it would almost seem that, for Shakespeare, gifting the world with the most extraordinary body of work that any author had produced before was merely a means to an end—and that end was retirement to the country town where he had been raised, no longer the idle son of an embarrassed glover, but a rich man, armigerous gentleman, respectable, boring, and thoroughly middle class.

There are no contemporary accounts of precisely how Shakespeare died, but the vicar of the church where he was buried recorded in his diary that, "Shakespeare, Drayton, and Ben Jonson had a merry meeting and it seems drank too hard, for Shakespeare died of a fever there contracted." It is quite possible that Drayton and Johnson came to Stratford to visit their old friend, but it seems unlikely that Shakespeare contracted a fever from drinking alcohol. People in the early 17th century routinely died of diseases of which fever was a primary symptom, particularly typhus, and there was a recorded outbreak of typhus in Shakespeare's neighborhood around the time of his death. Furthermore, C. Martin Mitchell, author of a biography about Dr. John C. Hall, who was married to Shakespeare's older daughter Susanna, has yet another explanation for Shakespeare's final illness:

> "I have formed the opinion that it was more likely than not in the nature of a cerebral

hemorrhage or apoplexy that quickly deepened and soon became fatal. There are three reasons for this. Firstly, the hurried reconstruction and inter-lineated clauses of the Will not allowing time for it to be copied afresh before signature; Secondly, the earliest and clearest impressions of the Droeshout frontispiece of the First Folio show outstanding shadings, suggesting marked thickening of the left temporal artery– a sign of atheroma and arterio-sclerosis; and thirdly, such a termination is quite common in men who have undergone such continuous mental and physical strain over a prolonged period as our actor-manager-dramatist must have been subjected to throughout his, undoubtedly, strenuous career. Richard Burbage who daily shared the same theatrical life, himself died of such a seizure after twenty-four hours illness."

William Shakespeare died on April 23, 1616, within a few days of his fifty-second birthday. He was buried in the chancel of Holy Trinity Church on May 5th. The inscription on his tomb, thought to have been composed by Shakespeare himself, reads,

> Good friend for Jesus sake forbeare,
> To dig the dust enclosed here.
> Blessed be the man that spares these stones,
> And cursed be he that moves my bones.

The inscription scarcely seems like the work of a poetic genius. But perhaps, after such a long and storied career, he had already said everything he had to say.

Other books available by Michael W. Simmons on Kindle, paperback and audio:

Nikola Tesla: Prophet Of The Modern Technological Age

Albert Einstein: Father Of the Modern Scientific Age

Alexander Hamilton: First Architect of the American Government

Thomas Edison: American Inventor

Elizabeth I: Legendary Queen Of England

Further Reading

Will in the World: How Shakespeare Became Shakespeare, by Stephen Greenblatt

The Romance of Yachting, by Joseph C. Hart

    https://archive.org/stream/romanceofyachtin48hart/romanceofyachtin48hart_djvu.txt

The Holinshed Project

    http://www.cems.ox.ac.uk/holinshed/

Works of Raphael Holinshed

    http://www.gutenberg.org/ebooks/author/5166

"Is Shakespeare Dead?", by Mark Twain

https://ebooks.adelaide.edu.au/t/twain/mark/is_shakespeare_dead/chapter3.html

"To the Memory of My Beloved, the Author, Mr. William Shakespeare and What He Hath Left Us", by Ben Jonson

https://www.poetryfoundation.org/poems-and-poets/poems/detail/44466

"Some Account of the Life, &tc., of Mr. William Shakespear," by Nicholas Rowe

http://www.gutenberg.org/files/30227/30227-pdf.pdf

"Shakespeare and Religion", by Aldous Huxley

http://www.sirbacon.org/links/huxley2.htm

Palladis Tamia, by Francis Meres

http://www.bartleby.com/359/31.html

"Inter-acting: Marlowe and Shakespeare" by Humphrey Tompkin

http://uhaweb.hartford.edu/tonkin/pdfs/interacting.

Made in the USA
Middletown, DE
26 November 2023